500 RECIPES
ELECTRIC MIXERS AND BLENDERS

500 RECIPES
ELECTRIC MIXERS AND BLENDERS

Marguerite Patten

PAUL HAMLYN

LONDON · NEW YORK · SYDNEY · TORONTO

Contents

© Copyright The Hamlyn Publishing Group Limited 1969
Published by The Hamlyn Publishing Group Limited
London · New York · Sydney · Toronto
Hamlyn House · Feltham · Middlesex · England
Printed in England by Petty and Sons Limited, Leeds
SBN 600 03436 4

Introduction

Once upon a time a mixer might have been considered a luxury in the kitchen, unless a great deal of cake making, etc., was carried out, for it consisted of a bowl and whisk which was admirable for creaming and whisking, but of little value for other purposes. Today this is not true, for mixers have been made to suit homes of all kinds. There are the large mixers which, with their various attachments, cover the majority of the 'chores' connected with the preparation of food—whisking, creaming, emulsifying, mincing, etc., as well as slicing, shredding and peeling potatoes. In addition, there is a wide selection of smaller models (portable or hand mixers, as they are generally described); while these are considerably less expensive and smaller and in consequence will deal with smaller quantities of food, they are invaluable in whisking, beating, etc., and may be used in any bowls, put into saucepans, etc.

One of the most interesting developments in kitchen appliances in recent years is the blender or liquidiser. In most cases this will take the place of a sieve and it blends or emulsifies food within a matter of seconds.

I have enjoyed compiling this book, for I was concerned with testing some of the earliest mixers, have watched the improvement over the years and have tried to convince many people that mixers and blenders *do* save a great deal of time, trouble and *money*, as well as enabling you to prepare dishes that normally could be too complicated for a busy housewife. I hope you find the hints and recipes helpful.

Marguerite Patten

Useful facts and figures

Comparison of English and American weights and measurements

English weights and measures have been used throughout this book. 3 teaspoonfuls equal 1 tablespoon. The average English teacup is $\frac{1}{4}$ pint or 1 gill. The average English breakfast cup is $\frac{1}{2}$ pint or 2 gills.

When cups are mentioned in recipes they refer to a B.S.I. measuring cup which holds $\frac{1}{2}$ pint or 10 fluid ounces. The B.S.I. standard tablespoon measures 1 fluid ounce.

In case it is wished to translate any of the weights and measures into their American, Canadian or French counterparts, the following tables give a comparison.

Liquid measure

The most important difference to be noted is that the American and Canadian pint is 16 fluid ounces, as opposed to the British Imperial pint, which is 20 fluid ounces. The American $\frac{1}{2}$-pint measuring cup is therefore actually equivalent to two-fifths of a British pint. In Australia the British Imperial pint, 20 fluid ounces, is used.

Solid measure

English		American
1 lb. Butter or other fat		2 cups
1 lb. Flour		4 cups
1 lb. Granulated or Castor Sugar		2 cups
1 lb. Icing or Confectioner's Sugar		3 cups
1 lb. Brown (moist) Sugar		$2\frac{1}{2}$ cups
1 lb. Golden Syrup or Treacle		1 cup
1 lb. Rice		2 cups
1 lb. Dried Fruit		2 cups
1 lb. Chopped Meat (finely packed)		2 cups
1 lb. Lentils or Split Peas		2 cups
1 lb. Coffee (unground)		$2\frac{1}{2}$ cups
1 lb. Soft breadcrumbs		4 cups
$\frac{1}{2}$ oz. Flour	1 level tablespoon*	
1 oz. Flour	1 heaped tablespoon	
1 oz. Sugar	1 level tablespoon	
$\frac{1}{2}$ oz. Butter	1 level tablespoon smoothed off	
1 oz. Golden Syrup or Treacle	1 level tablespoon	
1 oz. Jam or Jelly	1 level tablespoon	

*must be standard measuring tablespoon.

French weights and measures

It is difficult to convert to French measures with absolute accuracy, but 1 oz. is equal to approximately 30 grammes, 2 lb. 3 oz. to 1 kilogramme. For liquid measure, approximately $1\frac{3}{4}$ English pints may be regarded as equal to 1 litre; 1 demilitre is half a litre, and 1 decilitre is one-tenth of a litre.

Description of oven	Approximate temperature centre of oven °F	Thermostat Setting
Very slow or		$\frac{1}{4}=240$
Very cool	200–250	$\frac{1}{2}=265$
		$1=290$
Slow or Cool	250–300	$2=310$
Very Moderate	300–350	$3=335$
Moderate	350–375	$4=350$
Moderately Hot		$5=375$
to Hot	375–400	$6=400$
Hot to Very Hot	425–450	$7=425$
Very Hot	450–500	$8=450$
		$9=470$

Note: This table is an approximate guide only. Different makes of cooker vary and if you are in any doubt about the setting it is as well to refer to the manufacturer's temperature chart. Australian gas oven temperatures are often in °F. Use 50°F. *less* for gas than electricity.

Types of mixers and attachments

There is a wide selection of mixers (plus various attachments—see page 11) and blenders (liquidisers) on the market. If you are thinking of buying a model, there are certain points to consider:

1 Would the amount of use justify a large model or would it be wiser to invest in a small portable one?
2 Do you need this for whisking, creaming, etc., or for sieving, chopping—if the former then a mixer is necessary, if the latter then a liquidiser would be of more value, and if you need help with all these tasks, then buy a combined model.

To make the best use of a mixer

a Instructions
Read the instructions given by the manufacturer.

b Servicing
Note carefully any instructions about servicing and if this should be carried out at regular intervals. Fill in any guarantee card supplied with the mixer.

c Cleaning
Note instructions about cleaning mixer and whether there are parts that must not be immersed in water or made damp; dry blades on mincers very well.

d Capacity
Never exceed the capacity of the mixer—too much food in a mixing bowl or liquidiser goblet puts an undue strain on the motor.

e Timing
Never run the motor for longer than the period specified by the manufacturer.

f Storing mixer
A mixer is of far less value if 'tucked away' in a cupboard, for it means time and effort in getting it out. Try to have a mixer in such a position that it can be used *at once*. There are often plastic covers obtainable, so it can be covered when not in use.
Often portable mixers can be put into a support on the wall. Make sure whisks are not bent in any way.

Using an electric mixer

An electric mixer, whether a large model or a small hand appliance, is one of the biggest aids in the kitchen. It must be stressed, however, that this is a general book and that detailed instructions for the use of *your* particular mixer should be noted from the manufacturer's instruction booklet. In some cases, quantities given in a recipe may seem a little large for a small mixer, in this case it is better to use half quantity and prepare that and then repeat the process with the remaining ingredients. **Never try to mix too great a quantity of food at one time.** If the mixer, whatever its size, seems incapable of coping with the amount of mixture, you have probably got too much in the bowl.

How does a mixer work?

The blade or blades or whisk attachment moves at a fairly high speed so taking the place of a hand whisk or wooden spoon.
When making cakes can the fat be used when hard?
Many modern fats never become very hard and they should cream quite easily. If however the butter, margarine or cooking fat is rather firm, the mixer will be more efficient if the mixing bowl is warmed before the fat is put into this. Do not melt or over warm the fat itself otherwise insufficient air will be beaten into the mixture.
When making a cake may the flour be added with the mixer?
This very much depends upon (a) the type of mixer, a small hand mixer used on a low speed is far less vigorous than a really big mixer, but (b) far more important it depends upon the type of cake. An ordinary family economical cake may have the flour blended with the mixer, but a really light sponge or rich cake could be spoiled by using a more energetic action of an electric mixer. To sum up, therefore, one uses a mixer for creaming fat and sugar then adding eggs, or whisking eggs and sugar but it is wiser to put the flour in by hand.

Is it necessary to have a mixer serviced?
See the comments on page 7.

What speed is needed for using the mixer with the greatest efficiency?
This will vary with the kind of food being mixed and also the variation of speeds on the particular model. Most detailed advice is given under the various recipes but the general rule is, use a slow speed for creaming fats, etc., use a higher speed for a whisking action for egg whites, eggs and sugar, cream (do be very careful not to over whisk).

What kind of recipes should one use for a mixer?
Really there is no need to have special recipes, you can use your own favourites, but those in this book give you ideas for making the best use of the appliance.

For example you can:

a Cream fat and sugar for cakes, puddings, etc. see page 72.

b Mix fat and flour for pastry, scones, etc. see page 65.

c Cream cooked vegetables such as potatoes, etc.

d Whisk eggs and sugar or egg whites for cakes, meringues, etc. see pages 52 and 72.

e Whisk jellies for special desserts, see page 49.

f Whisk cream or cream mixture, see page 54.

g Make mayonnaise or sauces based on a mayonnaise, see pages 46–48.

Using a blender or liquidiser

A blender or liquidiser, as it is often called, can be one of the attachments on a mixer or it can be an entirely separate appliance. In the case of the larger models its capacity can be over 2 pints or with smaller models it will be 1 pint or even slightly less. In spite of these differences, however, the basic principles on which a blender works and the way it should be used are the same.

Obviously when using a small model with fairly large quantities of food you will need to fill and re-fill the goblet several times, but the blender works so quickly that this will not be a great inconvenience.

How does a blender work?

The 'blades' at the bottom of the goblet revolve at a very great speed so 'breaking down' or emulsifying the ingredients until they become very fine particles or a smooth purée.

Can hot as well as cold ingredients be put into the blender goblet?
Yes. The blender goblet is designed to withstand heat, but it is important to warm the goblet before you pour in any hot ingredients.

The speed of blending
At the top of recipes in this book is the suggested speed on which to set the blender. If you are using a blender without a range of speeds, do not be worried by these instructions, but in the larger blenders one is able to move from a low to high speed—the power on high speed is very great and that is why it is better to use low speed for some mixtures, otherwise the result is not satisfactory or one gets unnecessary splashing against the side of the goblet.

The speed of mixers
At the top of recipes, you will find the suggested speed of mixing. If by chance you have a small hand mixer with little if any choice of speed, do not let this worry you, for you can still use the recipes on your setting. However, in the larger mixers there is quite a range of speeds and it is important to use the right speed for each recipe, otherwise food tends to be swept against the sides of the bowl rather than being kept in the base of the bowl where it is needed.

Are there any rules about the way the goblet is filled?

It is important to remember that liquids rise up in the goblet when the power is switched on, so it is important that the goblet is never more than two-thirds full—this is particularly important with very liquid mixtures—soups, drinks, etc. When making stuffings, sandwich fillings and pâtés the goblet does not operate if too much food is put in—see pages 13 and 32 for an example of the way to fill the goblet in these circumstances.

How does one clear the goblet?

Generally one can clear the goblet like an ordinary container but if it has been used for very sticky mixtures—mayonnaise—pâté, etc., remove the maximum amount of food then half fill the goblet with hot water and a little detergent—switch on and these particles of food will be removed from the blades and base of the goblet.

Is it necessary to have a blender serviced?
See the comments on page 7.

What speed is needed for using the blender with the greatest efficiency?

This will vary with the kind of food being put into the goblet and also the variation of speeds on the particular model—most detailed advice is given under the various recipes.

What kind of recipes should one use for a blender?

Really there is no need to have *special* recipes, you can use your own favourites, but those in this book give you ideas for making the best use of the appliance.

For example you can:

a Make a purée of vegetables, etc., for soups, to add to stews, etc.
There are many recipes under the soup section, see page 15.

b Make fruit purées for sauces, desserts, ice creams, etc., see pages 49 and 55.

c Make a lumpy sauce quite smooth again, or emulsify the ingredients for various sauces, one of the most successful being a mayonnaise, see page 34.

d Make excellent sandwich fillings and various kinds of pâté, see page 13.

e Make milk shakes and other drinks—adding ice and fresh fruit, etc., see pages 84–85.

f Prepare various stuffings, see pages 32–33.

g 'Chop' dry ingredients such as bread for breadcrumbs, cheese, parsley, etc.

h Cope with unexpected shortages in the cupboard, e.g. turn ordinary sugar into icing sugar, blanched almonds into ground almonds, see page 10.

Use of the lid

In some recipes it is suggested that the cap in the lid is removed or the lid of the blender goblet tilted. The object of this is to add ingredients gradually while the motor is in operation.

Many lids do not have a removable cap and before making mayonnaise or any other recipe where the lid has to be tilted, it is advisable to 'practise' with a little water in the goblet and see at which angle you can hold the lid so there is no splashing.

The blender for dry ingredients

One of the most valuable tasks done by the blender (liquidiser) in the kitchen is to 'chop' dry foods, e.g. here are some that may be chopped. A medium speed is generally advisable.

Bread to make breadcrumbs

Do not try to put in too much bread at one time. Drop in several pieces with the motor running (medium speed), continue to add the bread until as fine as required. STOP adding bread the moment the blades seem unable to make fine crumbs—this is your signal that sufficient bread has been added. The fresher the bread the smaller the amount that can be turned into crumbs at one time, but remember it takes about 20 seconds only.

Crisp breadcrumbs

Add small pieces of crisped bread and then switch on, there is no need to add crisped bread gradually, it can be put into the goblet, then the motor switched on.

Biscuits, corn flakes, cake, etc., may be turned into crumbs in the same way.

Cheese

Cut cheese into 1 inch cubes—very hard Parmesan should be cut into smaller pieces—and feed gradually into the dry goblet. With smaller mixers it may be better to put all the cheese into the goblet before switching on—with larger goblets, remove cap from lid or tilt the lid itself, switch to medium speed and add cheese. The moment the cheese becomes sticky, switch off, empty out the cheese and start again.

Coffee

See comments on right. Put a small quantity of coffee beans into the dry goblet, switch on to medium speed and leave until ground to the desired fineness.

Herbs

Parsley, mint and other herbs may be chopped as garnish or to add to dishes.
Add gradually to the dry goblet with the motor on medium speed. For very fine cut herbs add a little water to the goblet, put in the sprigs of parsley, etc., leave until as fine as required, then strain carefully and dry if necessary by spreading out on plates, etc.

Nuts

Add the nuts gradually to the dry goblet on low speed and leave until as fine as desired; watch carefully for the nuts become very fine in a very short time. For coarsely cut nuts add gradually to the goblet with the motor in action. See above right for making ground almonds.

Vegetables

Cut the vegetables into about 1 inch cubes and drop gradually into the dry goblet, switch on and watch carefully to make sure the vegetables do not become a pulp too quickly. For very finely chopped vegetables· add a little water to the goblet, put in the vegetables and leave until very fine, strain off liquid if not required for the specific recipe.

Your blender in an emergency

A blender can often be used for preparing extra foods from ingredients in the larder, for example:

Almonds—ground

First 'blanch' the nuts. Put them into boiling water, leave for a short time then remove skins and dry. Put into dry goblet, switch to low or medium and leave until finely and evenly ground. Many Continental recipes, e.g. the cake on page 73 use ground unblanched almonds; the skins will grind down as well as the nuts. Other nuts can be ground in the same way.

Butter—from cream

This can only be prepared in a blender where there is a low speed. Put in the cream, switch to low and leave until 'lumps of butter' form. Tip out of the goblet, use the liquid for mixing cakes, etc. Add a little salt to the 'butter'. Really good cream from the top of the milk can be used also.

Coffee—ground

First read directions for YOUR particular blender, for many manufacturers do NOT recommend grinding hard coffee beans in the blender—they often provide a grinder or grinding attachment. However, in an emergency most blenders are suitable. Put in a small amount of coffee beans, switch to low or medium speed and leave until as fine as required—a medium ground coffee is the most usual and useful—this is ideal for most percolators. If left sufficiently long the coffee beans can become as fine as instant coffee powder.

Sugar—icing

Granulated or castor sugar can be put into the dry goblet, the motor switched to low or medium and the sugar turned into 'icing' sugar. The colour may not be as perfect as the commercially prepared icing sugar, so try and tint the icing if possible.

Other attachments for your mixer

Some mixers have special attachments that may be added to the basic mixer as and when required—the blender has been described separately—see page 8. On the other hand, some of these, like a coffe grinder (mill) can be obtained as a separate appliance.

Can opener
To take the place of a hand opener.

Colander and sieve
For straining fruits, etc., with pips and stones. Ideal for invalid diets or babies.

Grinder
To grind coffee beans; can also be used for hard crusts of bread, etc. This attachment may also be known in some machines as the coffee grinder or mill. Make sure you follow the directions for quantity of beans, etc., for these are very hard and too great a quantity could damage the blades of the grinder or coffee mill.

Juice extractor
To remove juice from citrus fruits.

Juice separator
This is quite different from the juice extractor, for it separates the juice from all fruits, carrots, parsley and is invaluable for health diets, see page 91.

Mincer
To take the place of a hand mincer. Care must be taken in using this that food is not 'fed' into the mincer too quickly and that the food is pushed down with the right attachment—generally a solid wooden 'pusher'. **Never use your fingers to push food down while the mincer is in operation.** If mincing a variety of ingredients for a recipe, put in drier food (e.g. meat) first, then end with more moist ingredients (e.g. onion).

Potato peeler
To remove peel or skins from potatoes. Naturally, the best result is obtained if you choose similar sized potatoes.

Slicer and shredder
This slices cucumber, potatoes, etc. into wafer-thin slices; it may also be used for grating cheese, carrots, shredding suet, etc.

Other attachments you may hear about are an oil dripper, bean slicer, pea 'podder', etc.

Hors d'œuvre

An interesting hors d'œuvre can turn a family meal into a special occasion menu. Often a home made pâté, mousse, etc., may be prepared from ingredients that might have been wasted. Salads—page 45 and some of the fish dishes—page 22 make excellent hors d'œuvre. Serve half portions if this is followed by a substantial main dish.

Oeufs à la crème

cooking time   10 minutes
mixer speed   low

you will need for 4 servings:

3 eggs	seasoning, pinch curry
3 oz. cooked ham	powder
½ small green pepper	heart of a lettuce
¼ pint thick cream	
3 tablespoons mayonnaise	

to garnish:
chopped parsley   paprika pepper

1 Hard boil the eggs for 10 minutes, crack shell and plunge into cold water to prevent dark line forming round the egg yolks.
2 Meanwhile dice ham finely and dice the green pepper, discard core and seeds.
3 Put cream into bowl, whisk until it just holds its shape, add mayonnaise, seasoning, curry powder.
4 Fold in the chopped eggs, pepper and ham.
5 Shred the lettuce finely, put into glasses or small dishes, pile egg mixture on this and garnish with parsley and paprika.

Avocado pears Indienne

cooking time   few minutes
blender speed   medium

you will need for 4 servings:

1 good sized slice bread without crusts	2 tablespoons mayonnaise
1–1½ teaspoons curry powder	2 ripe avocado pears
	1 oz. butter
4 oz. prawns or shrimps	

1 Put pieces of bread into blender goblet with half curry powder, switch on until fine crumbs.
2 Blend prawns with mayonnaise and rest of curry powder.
3 Halve pears, remove stones, fill with prawns, top with crumbs and curry powder and the butter (in small pieces).
4 Brown under grill.

Avocado pears with lobster cream

mixer speed   low

you will need for 4 servings:

2 large ripe avocado pears	4 tablespoons cream
1 lemon	3 tablespoons mayonnaise
1 small lobster or small can lobster	seasoning

1 Halve the avocado pears, remove stone, sprinkle with lemon juice to keep flesh white.
2 Flake fish, put the cream and mayonnaise into bowl, whip until just stiff, add squeeze of lemon juice, seasoning and fish.
3 Pile on to avocado pears.

Fish cream

cooking time   15 minutes
blender speed   medium
mixer speed   low then high

you will need for 8 servings:
(or 4 as a light main dish)

1 lb. white fish (free from skin and bones or use canned tuna or salmon)	seasoning
1 oz. butter	2 tablespoons sherry
1 oz. flour	2 eggs
½ pint milk	¼ pint thick cream
½ oz. powder gelatine	

to garnish:
cucumber, tomato, lemon, lettuce

1 Cook the fish very lightly with seasoning and ½ pint water, strain the fish and put it into the blender goblet. Retain fish stock.
2 Make the sauce: heat butter, stir in flour, cook for several minutes then blend in milk. Bring to boil, cook until thickened. Add to the fish.
3 Dissolve gelatine in ¼ pint hot fish stock, add to other ingredients in blender.
4 Switch on until a smooth thick mixture, add sherry.
5 Whisk egg yolks until thick and creamy, add the fish mixture, stir until blended, allow to cool and begin to thicken.
6 Fold in lightly whipped cream, then stiffly whisked egg whites. Put into mould and allow to set.
7 Turn out and garnish.
   If preferred the fish may be flaked—this gives a less smooth mixture.

Variations

Lobster cream: Use flaked lobster instead of white fish, simmer the lobster shells with water to give the ¼ pint fish stock at Stage 3.
Ham cream: (excellent for hors d'œuvre if main course is fish.) Use cooked ham instead of fish and white stock at Stage 3.

Chicken cream: (more suitable for light main course.) Use chicken and chicken stock at Stage 3.

Stuffed tomatoes

Choose 4 large firm but ripe tomatoes, cut slice from the end opposite the stalk mark (this makes sure they stand upright). Scoop out centre pulp. Arrange stuffed tomatoes on bed of salad.

1 Put the pulp, 4 oz. cooked ham, 1 hard boiled egg, shake pepper into blender goblet, switch to medium until smooth. Pile into tomato cases. Either serve cold or heat for about 10 minutes in moderately hot oven. Garnish with rings of stuffed olive.

2 Make mayonnaise as page 47, leave about 3 tablespoons in goblet, add pulp from tomatoes, 2 gherkins, 2 teaspoons capers, switch to medium until smooth, blend with 4 oz. prawns. Pile into tomato cases, serve cold garnished with tiny pieces of lemon.

3 Put about 2 oz. bread into blender, make breadcrumbs, tip into basin, blend with 3 oz. cream cheese. Put centres from the tomatoes into the blender, add crumbs, and make smooth pulp, season well, pile into tomato cases. Serve cold or heat for 10 minutes in moderately hot oven. Garnish with rings of gherkin.

Shellfish cocktails

Make the tomato mayonnaise as page 47, if wished add a very little thick cream and lemon juice or for a piquant flavour add a few drops Worcestershire sauce or chilli sauce.

Blend the shelled prawns, flaked lobster or crab meat with the sauce and put on a bed of very finely shredded lettuce. Serve in glasses with a teaspoon.

Allow good $\frac{1}{4}$ pint sauce and 4–6 oz. prepared fish for 4 people. A small amount of diced red and/or green pepper, and little chopped celery gives a pleasant texture to this.

Pâtés, sandwich spreads

These can be made very quickly and are extremely satisfactory.

Pieces of meat, liver, etc., should be kept reasonably small.

If you want a pâté with small pieces of the liver, as that given on page 14 add in the order given.

For a perfectly smooth pâté or spread, all the ingredients may be added together.

A pâté or sandwich spread must be sufficiently stiff to hold a shape or spread, but if the initial mixture is too firm a great deal can be wasted in the goblet, that is why it is advisable to emulsify the HOT ingredients, for this will melt the butter or fat used and give a seemingly liquid mixture while hot which sets and becomes firm when cold.

In this way wastage is reduced to a minimum, for sandwich fillings see page 69.

Warning: Read comments about bones, etc., under soups.

Chicken liver pâté

cooking time 5–10 minutes
blender speed low

you will need for 4 servings:

8 oz. chickens' livers
1 small onion
clove garlic (optional)
3 oz. butter
seasoning

1 tablespoon brandy or
hot stock

to garnish:
lettuce, lemon

1 Cut the livers into halves.
2 Chop the onion, crush the garlic.
3 Fry together in the hot butter until just softened, do not over-cook the liver.
4 Put a little of the mixture including all the butter into the goblet while warm, switch to low.
5 As soon as this begins to soften add the rest of the ingredients.
6 If by chance the mixture seems to be a little too stiff for the blades then gradually add a little more hot stock. By using the ingredients while hot the butter is kept soft and the mixture is easier to blend.
7 Tip out into a buttered container.
8 Allow to cool.
9 Serve with hot toast, butter and garnish with lettuce and lemon.

Cream chicken liver pâté

Use above recipe, but omit the tablespoon stock or brandy and use thick cream —for a very soft pâté use recipe exactly as above, but add 2 tablespoons whipped cream to the pâté when it is emulsified, blend this in carefully, taste and add extra seasoning as required.

Goose liver pâté

This is of course considered the finest pâté of all—pâté de foie gras as it should be correctly called.
Use either of the above recipes replacing chickens' liver with goose liver, increasing the amount of seasoning, do not use too much onion for the fine flavour of the liver should be appreciated.

Liver pâté

cooking time 1¼ hours
mincer speed medium
or blender speed low to medium

you will need for 6–8 servings:

1 lb. calf's or lamb's liver
4–6 oz. bacon or fairly
fat pork

1 very small onion (optional)
1 clove garlic (optional)

for the sauce:
1 oz. butter
1 oz. flour
¼ pint milk
2 tablespoons sherry or
brandy

seasoning
4 tablespoons thick cream
or stock
2 eggs

to coat tin:
1 oz. butter

to top the pâté:
about 4–5 thin rashers
bacon
2–3 oz. butter

Method 1 with mincer:

1 Cut liver and bacon or pork into pieces, feed through mincer, for a fine smooth pâté mince twice and use finest blades; for a coarse cut pâté use coarser blades and mince once.
2 Mince onion and crush the garlic.
3 Make a thick sauce with butter, flour and milk, add sherry or brandy and seasoning, blend with liver, bacon and onion. Continue as Stage 4.

Method 2 with blender:

1 DO NOT ATTEMPT to put liver and bacon into goblet without any liquid.
2 First make sauce, add sherry or brandy, put into goblet. Mince onion, crush garlic.
3 Gradually add liver, bacon and onion, leave until smooth. Continue as Stage 4.

Whether using methods 1 or 2 continue as follows:

4 Blend with garlic, cream, or use stock for a darker pâté and add eggs.
5 Butter baking dish well, put in pâté, smooth flat, cover with bacon rashers (or very well-buttered paper).
6 Stand in another dish of cold water, so bottom and sides of pâté do not dry.

7 Bake for 1¼ hours in centre of a very moderate oven (300–350° F.—Gas Mark 3).
8 Leave in dish to cool, remove bacon if wished, top with 2–3 oz. melted butter.

Variations
For a less creamy pâté use stock in the sauce instead of milk.
Add 2–3 gherkins, a good pinch mixed herbs.
Piquant pâté—Omit sauce and use 4–6 oz. cream cheese.

Fish pâté
Use recipe for liver pâté, but mince 1¼ lb. white fish instead of liver.

Kipper pâté
Put uncooked flesh from 2 large kippers with 3 oz. hot melted butter, 1 spring onion or clove garlic, shake pepper into blender goblet, switch to medium until smooth, OR cream butter with mixer, add flaked kipper meat, finely chopped onion or crushed clove garlic and pepper. Cream slowly together.

Cod's roe pâté
Use about 12 oz. smoked cod's roe in place of kipper flesh.

To serve pâté
Serve with hot toast and butter.

To store pâté
A pâté is a highly perishable food, so must be stored in a cool place for a limited period only. In order to keep the top of the pâté quite moist it is advisable to melt 1–2 oz. butter and to pour this over the pâté when in the storage container.
When serving the pâté this layer of butter may be removed or it may be served with the pâté itself.

Making soups

On the following pages are a number of various soups that are so quickly and easily made in a blender goblet.
You can however continue to use your own favourite recipes as well but remember if short of time, the vegetables cook more quickly and retain greater flavour if you put them into the blender with some of the liquid *BEFORE* cooking. Onions have a slightly over-strong flavour, so use less onions than in your recipe, but other vegetables are excellent. You will not have as smooth a purée, though, as when the vegetables are put into the blender after cooking.
When tomatoes are part of the ingredients you still retain tiny particles of skin and the pips, and celery is still a little 'stringy', so soups containing these foods would need sieving if you require a perfectly smooth purée. Fish, meat and chicken soups can be made into a creamy consistency by pouring the mixture into the blender . . . take great care there are no bones that could harm the blades at the base of the goblet.

Warning: Warm the blender before adding very hot mixtures.
Do not overfill the goblet with the ingredients.
Make sure the lid is very firmly in position and hold this as you switch on.

Fruit soups
A fruit soup is an unusual as well as a delicious first course, particularly in hot weather, when the refreshing flavour is ideal.
Never make the mixture too sweet, for a fruit soup should sharpen one's appetite for the meal ahead.

Apple soup

cooking time	20 minutes
blender speed	high

you will need for 4 servings:

1 lb. apples (weight when peeled) — use fairly sharp cooking apples

1 pint water
½ pint white wine
sugar to taste

to garnish:
powdered cinnamon OR lemon rings

1 Slice and core apples.
2 Simmer in the water until tender.
3 Add the white wine.
4 Taste and stir in required sugar while the apple mixture is still sufficiently warm to make it dissolve completely.
5 Tip into the warmed blender goblet and switch gradually to high until smooth.
6 Either serve very hot topped with powdered cinnamon or very cold garnished with lemon rings.
This is typical of fruit soups, so popular on the Continent.

Soups that need no cooking

All quantities for 4–5 servings

Speedy gazpacho

Put 1 lb. skinned tomatoes, small piece green pepper, ¼ small skinned cucumber, 2 tablespoons olive oil, 1 crushed clove garlic into blender goblet, add seasoning, and ½ pint ice cold water, switch gradually to high until smooth. Serve very cold. A few spring onions can be added, also 1 oz. bread to thicken soup.

Frosted cheese soup

Put 1 pint cold milk, 4–6 oz. Cheddar cheese, small piece green pepper, small piece peeled cucumber into blender goblet, switch to medium until blended. Serve very cold.

Clear vegetable soup

Put 1½ pints very hot stock or canned consommé into hot blender goblet, add 2 chopped carrots, 2–3 spring onions (milder than ordinary onion), 1 small piece green pepper, small piece red pepper, small piece peeled cucumber, seasoning. Switch gradually to high until blended. Serve very hot.

Soups made in the blender

Cauliflower soup

Cook 1 medium cauliflower until just tender. Remove a few tiny sprigs for garnish. Save some of the liquid for the sauce. Cut the rest roughly and put into the blender goblet with 1 pint sauce made from 1 oz. butter, 1 oz. flour, 1 pint liquid (milk and cauliflower stock). Switch gradually to high until blended. Reheat the soup, add a little cream or extra knob butter and seasoning. Garnish with cauliflower sprigs and paprika. Serves 4–6.

Carrot soup

cooking time	10 minutes
blender speed	high

you will need for 4 servings:

8 small carrots
1 pint water
½ pint milk
1–2 chicken stock cubes

seasoning

to garnish:
chopped parsley or chives

1 As young carrots have much more flavour when under-cooked put all the ingredients into the blender goblet before cooking.
2 Switch gradually to high until smooth; OR if you wish to retain pieces of carrot, put the liquid into the goblet then add the carrots gradually until as smooth as wished.
3 Simmer, but do not allow to boil, or the appearance will be marred, for about 10 minutes — less if wished — then pour into soup cups and top with parsley or chives.
If using very old carrots, proceed as above, simmer for about 20 minutes, *then* add to blender goblet once again to make doubly certain soup is smooth.

Carrot and beef soup

Follow directions for carrot soup above, but use really good beef stock or consommé in place of water, milk and chicken stock cubes.

Carrot and sweet pepper soup

Proceed as carrot soup above, but add ½ small green pepper and ½ small red pepper at Stage 2 (these can be raw or cooked with the carrots).

Chestnut soup

cooking time	1 hour 10 minutes
blender speed	high

you will need for 4 servings:

1 lb. chestnuts	good pinch salt, cayenne
1 pint water or white	pepper, and sugar if liked
stock	
2 oz. margarine or butter	**to garnish:**
½ pint milk	chopped parsley
	croûtons (see page 18)

1 Split the skins of the chestnuts, cover with water and cook for 15 minutes.
2 Peel the nuts while still hot, then return to the saucepan with the water or stock.
3 Simmer gently for 45 minutes.
4 Put chestnuts and all the other ingredients in recipe into warmed blender goblet, switch gradually to high.
5 Reheat if necessary.
6 Pour into hot soup cups and top with garnish.

Chestnut and ham soup

Follow directions for the chestnut soup above, but cook in ham stock. Garnish with very finely diced lean ham.

Cucumber soup

Remove the peel from ¾ of a medium sized cucumber (this makes sure it is not too bitter). Cut the cucumber into pieces. Simmer in 1 pint chicken stock or water and stock cubes for 10–15 minutes with 1–2 leeks or onions. Put into blender goblet with sprig mint, ¼ pint thin cream and seasoning. Serve hot or cold.

Lentil soup

cooking time	1½ hours
blender speed	high

you will need for 4 servings:

8 oz. washed lentils	little chopped thyme or
4 oz. bacon	parsley
1 onion, chopped	1 oz. butter
1 carrot	½ oz. flour
1 pint water or stock	½ pint milk
seasoning	

to garnish:
chopped parsley

1 Put the lentils (these can be soaked overnight if wished), bacon, onion, carrot and stock into a saucepan and add seasoning and herbs—the seasoning MUST be added at the very start of cooking.
2 Cover and simmer gently for about 1½ hours.
3 Make a thin sauce with the butter, flour and milk.
4 When thickened put into the warmed blender goblet.
5 Add lentil mixture—switch gradually to high.
6 Leave until smooth.
7 Reheat if necessary, taste, add more seasoning if necessary and garnish.
   Note:
   If wished, omit the sauce and serve this as a less creamy soup.

Green pea soup

Use dried peas instead of lentils, flavour with a sprig fresh mint or good pinch dried mint while cooking.

Bean soup

Follow directions for lentil soup but use butter or haricot beans in place of lentils; soak overnight. Add 2 onions and 1 leek when cooking the beans.

Haricot bean and cheese soup

Follow directions for lentil soup but use haricot beans, soak these overnight. When soup is cooked proceed as recipe, but add 4 oz. Cheddar or better still Danish Blue cheese at Stage 6. Reheat with care, do not over-cook.

Potato soup

cooking time   just under 10 minutes
blender speed   high

you will need for 4 servings:

4 medium potatoes   1 pint water
1 small onion   1–2 chicken stock cubes
½ pint milk   seasoning
to garnish:
chopped chives or parsley

Method as Carrot soup on page 16.
Do not exceed the amount of onion unless pre-cooking this.

Creamed spinach soup

cooking time   25 minutes
blender speed   high

you will need for 4 servings:

1 lb. spinach or 1 small   1½ pints milk
   packet frozen spinach   2 egg yolks
1 oz. butter   3 tablespoons thick cream
1 small onion, sliced   nutmeg
1 oz. cornflour or 2 oz.   seasoning
   flour
to garnish:
croûtons (see below)

1 Cook the spinach.
2 Heat the butter in a saucepan and fry the onion until tender but not brown.
3 Add the cornflour or flour, mix well and cook for a few minutes.
4 Add the milk, stir until boiling and boil for 3 minutes.
5 Put the sauce, then the spinach into the warmed blender goblet and switch gradually to high speed until smooth.
6 Put in the egg yolks and cream when smooth and leave for 1–2 minutes, season well.
7 There is no need to reheat this, but if doing so, then use a low heat so the soup does not curdle.
8 Garnish with croûtons.

Croûtons

cooking time   few minutes

you will need:

bread   hot fat for frying

1 Cut bread into really small dice or other shapes.
2 Fry in hot fat until crisp and golden brown.
3 Drain on absorbent paper.

More cream soups

Ingredients as creamed spinach soup with the following modifications:

Creamed avocado soup

Use 2 large ripe avocado pears instead of spinach. Do not cook the avocado pears, remove the pulp, add to the ingredients at stage 5, and continue as recipe.

Creamed broccoli soup

Use cooked fresh or frozen broccoli instead of spinach.

Creamed cabbage soup

Use cooked cabbage instead of spinach, but increase the amount of onions to 2–3.

Cream of tomato soup

cooking time   1¼ hours
blender speed   high

you will need for 4 servings:

1 lb. tomatoes   little fat bacon
1 onion   1½ pints stock or water
1 carrot   seasoning
1 stick celery   *bouquet garni*
¼–½ pint milk   ¾ oz. cornflour or
pinch sugar   1½ oz. flour

to garnish:
chopped white of hard-
   boiled egg or croûtons
   (see left)

1 Slice the vegetables.
2 Fry the bacon slowly to extract the fat, then add the vegetables and fry for about 10 minutes.
3 Add the stock (or water), seasoning and *bouquet garni*, bring to the boil and simmer gently until tender – about 1 hour.
4 The *bouquet garni* could be removed or emulsified with the soup.
5 Put all the ingredients, including bacon, unless you wish to remove this, into the warmed blender goblet and blend until smooth; add the

cornflour or flour mixed with the milk, blend well.
6 Return to the pan, bring just to the boil, stirring well, and cook gently for 2–3 minutes.
7 Check seasoning, add the sugar and serve with chosen garnish.

If preferred, make the tomato purée and make a coating sauce with 1 oz. butter, 1 oz. flour, $\frac{1}{2}$ pint milk. Put the purée and the sauce into the warmed goblet and switch gradually to high, and emulsify. Serve at once or reheat gently.

Cream of vegetable soup

| cooking time | 45 minutes |
| blender speed | high |

you will need for 4 servings:

$1\frac{1}{4}$–$1\frac{1}{2}$ lb. mixed vegetables*	2 oz. butter
	$\frac{1}{2}$ oz. flour
1 pint water or white stock	$\frac{1}{4}$–$\frac{1}{2}$ pint milk
$\frac{1}{4}$ teaspoon vinegar	**to garnish:**
seasoning	paprika and/or parsley

*Choose a good selection: because only a small amount of flour is used, include 1 or 2 vegetables like potatoes and carrots which give thickening. Tomatoes and/or carrots will give colour. A small quantity of green vegetables can be added but avoid too many very strongly flavoured vegetables such as turnips—a mixed vegetable soup should have a good balance of flavours.

1 Wash and peel vegetables and cut into medium sized pieces.
2 Put into a saucepan with water or stock, vinegar and seasoning.
3 Simmer gently for a good 30 minutes.
4 Pour or spoon carefully into the warmed blender goblet and switch gradually to high until smooth.
5 Return purée to saucepan, adding the butter.
6 Blend the flour with the cold milk, stir into the boiling purée and continue cooking, stirring all the time, until it forms a smooth thick soup.
7 Garnish with paprika and/or parsley.

Note:
The seeds and minute particles of peel will still be present from the tomatoes, so these could be de-seeded before cooking or the purée could be poured through a strainer – this is only necessary for very small children or for invalids who must have no roughage of any kind.

Vegetable soup

| cooking time | 45 minutes |
| blender speed | high |

you will need for 4 servings:

Either use recipe for cream of vegetable soup, (below, left) omitting milk and using all stock or water or for a coarse soup continue as follows:

1 Use ingredients as cream of vegetable soup.
2 Put the stock into the blender goblet—this can be cold.
3 Gradually 'feed' the pieces of vegetable into this until as fine as required—see directions for use of lid, etc., on page 9 and comments about onions on page 15 when using this method.
4 Tip the vegetable mixture into pan and continue as cream of vegetable soup or omit milk and just use all stock.

Cream of mushroom soup

| cooking time | 5–10 minutes |
| blender speed | high |

you will need for 4 servings:

8 oz. mushrooms*	1 pint water or white stock
2 oz. butter or margarine	$\frac{3}{4}$ pint milk
2 oz. flour	seasoning

*Mushroom stalks can be used

1 Mushrooms retain so much more of their flavour if lightly cooked, so put the mushrooms into the dry goblet and switch on for a few seconds to chop; in this way, the cooking time will be cut to a minimum.
2 Melt margarine or butter in saucepan, fry mushrooms for 5 minutes, stirring to prevent their discolouring.
3 Stir in flour and cook for 3 minutes.
4 Remove the pan from the heat and gradually add water or stock and milk.
5 Bring to the boil and cook until soup thickens.
6 Season and return to warmed blender goblet for a very smooth soup, switching gradually to high.

Variations
Add $\frac{1}{4}$ pint thick cream to the soup at Stage 6.
Omit the milk and use $1\frac{1}{2}$ pints brown stock for a very savoury soup.

Watercress soup

cooking time   20 minutes
blender speed   high

you will need for 4 servings:

2 bunches watercress (about 4 oz. when stalks removed)
1 oz. butter or chicken fat
1 pint good white stock OR use water and chicken stock cube
$\frac{1}{2}$ oz. cornflour or 1 oz. flour
$\frac{1}{4}$ pint milk
seasoning
3 tablespoons thick cream

1 Wash the watercress, reserving some sprigs to garnish.
2 Fry slowly for 2–3 minutes in the heated butter or fat.
3 Add stock, bring to boiling point, stirring, then simmer about 10 minutes.
4 Do not overcook as this will lose the flavour of the watercress.
5 Mix the cornflour or flour smoothly with the milk.
6 Add to the watercress mixture. Cook for 5 minutes, stirring; add seasoning.
7 Put into warmed blender goblet, switch gradually to high and keep at this speed until the watercress is as fine as desired.
8 Just before serving stir in the cream and garnish with sprigs of watercress.

Creamed fish soup

cooking time   20 minutes
blender speed   high

you will need for 4 servings:

1 small onion
approximately 12 oz. fish —this can be all white fish or a mixture of white fish and smoked haddock
small bunch parsley
$\frac{1}{2}$ pint water
1 oz. butter
1 oz. flour
$\frac{1}{2}$ pint milk
seasoning

to garnish:
a little onion or cayenne or paprika pepper

1 Slice the onion and put with the fish and parsley into the water.
2 Simmer gently until just soft.
3 Put all these ingredients into blender goblet.
4 Switch on until smooth.
5 Meanwhile, make the sauce with the butter, flour and milk.

6 Add the fish mixture to the sauce and heat gently.
7 Taste and season, if wished return to blender goblet to make sure the sauce and fish mixture are emulsified.
8 Serve with chosen garnish.

Shellfish soups

If using fresh crab, lobster or prawns simmer the shells with $\frac{3}{4}$ pint water with a small onion and bunch parsley for 15 minutes, strain this carefully. Make a sauce with 1 oz. butter, 1 oz. flour, the fish stock, and $\frac{1}{2}$ pint milk. Put into the blender goblet with the flesh from a medium crab or lobster or about 6 oz. prawns (weight when shelled). Switch on until smooth, adding good pinch cayenne pepper, little sherry or brandy or white wine to flavour.
If using canned lobster or crab meat make the sauce with all milk, flavoured with a few drops anchovy essence, season very well and flavour with white wine.

Salmon or tuna soup

Canned or freshly cooked salmon or tuna may be used instead of white fish in the creamed fish soup. As these fish are more solid than white fish a good 8 oz. is sufficient.

Poultry and game soups

These may be made very economically with the carcass of the chicken or game.
To make approximately 3 pints soup (enough for 6–8 people). Put the carcass of a good sized chicken or 2 pheasants, etc., into a pan, cover with $3\frac{1}{2}$ pints water, seasoning, vegetables as wished—onions, carrots, etc., *bouquet garni*, then simmer gently for about 2–2$\frac{1}{2}$ hours in a covered saucepan. If preferred use a pressure cooker and allow 45 minutes only, use only 2$\frac{1}{2}$ pints liquid as there is no evaporation in cooking.
For an unthickened soup: Remove the bones from the stock, and take any tiny pieces of meat from the bones to add to the soup. Put the meat, vegetables and some of the stock into the hot blender goblet, switch gradually to high until smooth. Put into the saucepan,

and dilute with the rest of the stock, re-season and heat.

For a thickened soup: Blend 1½ oz. flour with a little of the stock, heat steadily, stirring well, add about 2 oz. butter as soup thickens.

For a creamed soup: Use only 2½ pints water in the saucepan then blend 1½ oz. flour with 1 pint milk, add to the purée, together with 2 oz. butter and bring to the boil, stirring well, cook until thickened.

To add flavour to the soup

For game soups . . . add port wine, little red-currant jelly.

For chicken soup . . . add sherry and a little thick cream (do not boil after adding this).

Mulligatawny soup

cooking time	1 hour
blender speed	high

you will need for 4 servings:

1 apple	2 pints stock*
1 large carrot	1 tablespoon chutney
2 onions	1 oz. sultanas
2 oz. fat or dripping	pinch sugar
1 oz. flour	seasoning
1 tablespoon curry powder	little lemon juice or vinegar

*Made by simmering lamb or mutton bones or a small lamb's head.

1 Chop apple and vegetables into small (NOT tiny) pieces, toss in the hot dripping, then work in the flour and curry powder.
2 Add the stock, bring to the boil and cook until thickened.
3 Add remaining ingredients and cook together for about 45 minutes–1 hour.
4 Put into warmed blender goblet, switch gradually to high until smooth.
5 Reheat if desired.
6 Taste, adjusting seasoning if necessary, and add sugar or lemon juice if required.

Low calorie mushroom soup

cooking time	5 minutes
blender speed	high

you will need for 4–5 servings:

8 oz. mushrooms or mushroom stalks	1½ pints stock (white or brown)
small bunch parsley	seasoning, including pinch cayenne pepper
1 small onion	
to garnish:	
chopped parsley or chives	

1 Simmer all ingredients for 5 minutes only.
2 Put into warmed blender goblet, switch on until smooth.
3 Serve, topped with more chopped parsley or chives.

Low calorie tomato soup

cooking time	few minutes
blender speed	high

you will need for 4–5 servings:

1 lb. tomatoes	1 pint white stock or water and chicken stock cubes
2 spring onions or about 1–2 tablespoons chives	seasoning

1 Skin the tomatoes, either by putting into very hot water for about 1 minute then into cold water and pulling off the skins, or by inserting a fine skewer or fork into the tomatoes and holding them over heat until the skin 'cracks'.
2 Put the tomatoes, onions or chives and a little stock into the blender goblet.
3 Switch gradually to high until a smooth purée.
4 Put into the saucepan, adding the rest of the stock.
5 Heat and season well.

Cold soups

Many soups are excellent served cold (see Speedy Gazpacho page 16, creamed soups, etc.). As the soup will thicken more as it cools use only half the amount of flour given in the recipe. *To prevent a skin forming* as the soup becomes cold pour a little thin cream or milk on top of the soup, stir this in before serving.

Jellied soups

A lightly jellied soup is delicious. Use any of the basic recipes in this chapter but omit any flour used in thickening. Instead use gelatine. *If the purée is fairly thick* when it comes from the blender then allow about ¼ oz. powder gelatine (2 teaspoons) to each pint. Dissolve the gelatine thoroughly in a little hot stock and add to the soup. *If the purée is very thick* 1 teaspoon per pint should be enough. *If a thin purée* then 3 teaspoons per pint. Spoon into cold soup cups and garnish with lemon, etc.

Iced soups

Follow directions for jellied soups, using slightly less gelatine. The use of gelatine prevents tiny 'splinters' of ice forming in the soup. Put into freezing trays and frost lightly. Do not allow to become too hard and iced.

Using the whisk for soups

Naturally the whisk has not been designed for 'sieving' soups, but where a soft vegetable like potatoes is the basis of the soup this can be done. The following recipe is a good basic one to use for this method of achieving a smooth soup.

Potato soup

cooking time	25 minutes
mixer speed	low

you will need for 4–5 servings:

12 oz. potatoes (weight when peeled)	1 pint stock or extra water and a stock cube
1 onion	2–3 tablespoons thick or thin cream
¾ pint water	1–2 oz. butter
seasoning	
bouquet garni	

to garnish:
chopped parsley or
   chopped chives or
   chopped watercress

1 Cook the potatoes with the onion in well seasoned water with the herbs until soft.
2 Strain off water—do not discard this, remove the onion and chop this finely—remove herbs.
3 Either mash the potatoes in the pan if using a portable mixer or transfer to a warmed bowl and whisk until smooth.
4 Return to the saucepan with the chopped onion then gradually blend in the potato stock and the extra stock or water and stock cube.
5 Taste and season well, reheat adding the cream and butter. Garnish.
Note:
This is a good basic way of making a smooth soup without sieving and where you have no blender.

Vegetable soup

Use the same recipe as for potato soup, choosing a good selection of vegetables, e.g. 1 potato, 1 carrot, 1–2 onions, few peas and/or beans and a small piece of cauliflower and 1 tomato. If you omit potato and carrot which help to thicken the soup, you will need to thicken by blending 1 oz. flour or ½ oz. cornflour (or little more if wished) with liquid and stirring this into the vegetable mixture at stage 5 BEFORE adding the cream or use any of the vegetable soups in this section, adapting the process to a mixer.

Fish dishes

In the past many fish dishes needed finely pounded fish to make them successfully—this tedious and time-consuming task can now be replaced by using a blender (liquidiser) or mincer. This chapter gives a number of delicious fish dishes made with the help of a mixer or its attachments.

Fish balls

cooking time	8 minutes
mincer speed	medium

you will need for 4–5 servings:

1 lb. white fish	seasoning
1 small onion	1 egg
2 oz. bread (without crusts)	

to coat:	**to deep fry:**
1 oz. seasoned flour	oil or fat
1 egg	
2 oz. soft breadcrumbs	

1 Put the skinned fish through the mincer, then the onion and the bread.
2 Season well and bind with an egg.
3 Form into about 12–16 small balls, coat in flour then egg and crumbs.
4 Test the oil or fat; a cube of bread should turn golden brown within 1 minute if using fat, ½ minute if using oil.
5 Put the fish balls into a frying basket and lower into the fat, reduce the heat so they do not brown too quickly on the outside, then fry

steadily until crisp and brown and cooked. Never try to cook too quickly, as the mixture must be cooked right through.

6 Drain on absorbent paper. Serve hot or cold with a hot sauce, tartare sauce and vegetables or salad.

Variations

Cooked fish, finely chopped or minced, could be used—then coat with browned breadcrumbs and shorten the cooking time.

Kipper balls

Put boned, uncooked kippers through the mincer—these are excellent for parties if made very small and served very hot. Season well with cayenne pepper.

Salmon balls

Use canned salmon—as this is a soft-textured fish it can be put into the blender goblet instead of the mincer—mix with the egg to make a softer mixture that is less likely to be wasted at the bottom of the blender. Add 1 or 2 small gherkins to give an interesting 'bite' to the mixture.

Shrimp and egg croquettes

cooking time   15 minutes
blender speed   medium

you will need for 4 servings:

2 oz. bread (weight without crusts)	**to coat:** 1 oz. seasoned flour
1 oz. butter	1 egg
1 oz. flour	2 oz. crisp breadcrumbs (raspings)
¼ pint milk	
seasoning	**to fry:**
2 eggs	little fat
½ pint shelled shrimps	**to garnish:** lemon, watercress or parsley

1 First put the bread into the blender goblet, switch on until fine crumbs, tip into a basin.
2 Make a thick sauce with the butter, flour and milk, season well.
3 Hard-boil then shell the eggs.
4 Put the sauce, eggs and shrimps into the blender goblet, switch gradually to medium until smoothly blended, blend with the crumbs.
5 Allow the mixture to cool and stiffen, then form into about 8 finger shapes.

6 Coat with the seasoned flour, then the egg and crumbs.
7 Fry in shallow fat (or use deep fat if more convenient) until crisp and golden brown.
8 Drain on absorbent paper, serve hot or cold, garnished with lemon, watercress or parsley.

Variations

Rice and shrimp croquettes

Follow the recipe above, but use 1 oz. rice and cook until soft in boiling salted water, drain then mix with rest of the ingredients.

Shrimp and vegetable croquettes

Omit the eggs and put ½ green pepper, small portion of skinned cucumber, few capers and 1 cooked carrot into the blender goblet, then add the shrimps.

White fish croquettes

Use cooked fish instead of shrimps and add a few drops tomato ketchup or anchovy essence to the sauce.

Plaice in savoury custard

cooking time   1 hour
blender speed   medium

you will need for 4 servings:

4 medium-sized fillets of plaice	2 eggs
seasoning	½ pint milk
½–1 oz. butter	2–3 oz. Cheddar cheese
	small sprig of parsley

1 Skin the fillets of plaice; to do this, insert the tip of a sharp knife under the skin at the tail end of each fillet and ease the fish away from the skin; if you dip the knife into a little salt the skin is removed more easily.
2 Put the fish into a well-buttered dish, season lightly.
3 Put the eggs, milk, tiny knob of butter left from greasing the dish, plus the cheese and parsley into the blender goblet, switch gradually to medium until well blended, season lightly.
4 Allow to stand for a short time for any bubbles to 'subside' from the top of the custard, pour over the fish and bake in the centre of a very moderate oven (300–350°F.—Gas Mark 3) until set. If the milk was cold when added to the eggs, etc., this will take approximately 1 hour, if hot about 45–50 minutes.

10 ways in which a blender can give more interesting fish dishes

1 Cheese coated fish
Put cornflakes and cheese into blender to make a new coating for fish before frying. Choose thin fillets that do not take too long to cook, to prevent cheese becoming over-cooked.

2 Speedy fish casserole
Put 8 oz. tomatoes, 1 carrot, 2–3 mushrooms and seasoning in blender, season well, make a smooth purée. Put into shallow saucepan and poach fish in this. Lift out fish, thicken sauce if wished—not really necessary.

3 Fish and tomato loaf
Put 2 oz. bread into blender to make crumbs. Tip into bowl. Fry 1 medium chopped onion in 1 oz. butter, put into blender with 2 skinned tomatoes, 1 egg, sprig parsley, pinch mixed herbs or fresh thyme. Steam or poach, then flake 1 lb. white or other fish, blend with the crumb and tomato mixture. Put into greased $1\frac{1}{2}$–2 lb. loaf tin, cover with greased paper and bake for approximately 1 hour in the centre of a moderate to moderately hot oven (350–400° F. —Gas Mark 4–5). Turn out and serve hot or cold.

4 Crusty fish and tomato loaf
Coat sides of the buttered tin with a generous layer of crisp breadcrumbs, crushed cornflakes or potato crisps (make these in the blender or grinder). Top loaf with layer of crumbs and 1 oz. melted butter. Put buttered paper on top very loosely, remove half way through cooking.

5 Fish and vegetable pie
Fry 1–2 chopped onions in 2 oz. butter, put into the blender with 2 skinned tomatoes and 3 tablespoons water. Season well, add herbs as required. Switch on until smooth purée. Put 1 lb. flaked fish into pie dish, add tomato and onion mixture, then cover with 1 lb. creamed potatoes—see page 41, or 6 oz. short crust pastry—see page 65, and bake in the centre of a moderately hot oven (400°F.—Gas Mark 5–6) until brown and the filling hot, approximately 35–40 minutes.

6 Cheese pie
Recipe above can be varied by using cheese sauce, see page 35, instead of tomato mixture.

7 Add sliced hard boiled eggs on top of the fish—either with cheese or tomato mixtures.

8 Bacon and fish pie
Prepare tomato mixture as above, fry and chop 3 rashers bacon and add to this in the pie dish.

9 Low calorie fish 'pie'
Prepare tomato mixture, using little if any butter (simmer onion in water instead of frying). Blend with fish then spoon into the pie dish. Bake for 15 minutes, covered with foil. Remove from the oven. Whisk 2 egg whites until very stiff, season generously. Pile over the fish. Return to the oven for a further 15 minutes until golden brown.

10 Cheese meringue pie
Prepare mixture as low calorie fish pie but add 2 oz. finely grated cheese to egg whites.

Meat and poultry dishes

There are many ways in which a mixer will give great variety in interesting and economical meat or poultry dishes.

a) Sauces for casserole dishes are prepared in minutes with the help of the blender.

b) Light soufflé mixtures are little trouble with the help of a whisk.

c) Left-over meat or poultry can be turned into really interesting meals with the help of a mincer (or sometimes the blender can be used —where suitable this is indicated).

Stews and casserole dishes

Chicken Ragoût

cooking time	see method Stage 10
blender speed	low then high

you will need for 4 people:

1 small jointed boiling fowl or chicken or portions of cooked poultry	approximately 12 small onions or shallots
1 oz. flour (see Stage 6)	8–12 oz. young carrots
seasoning	3 skinned tomatoes
bouquet garni	
2 oz. chicken fat or butter	½ pint stock or water if using cooked chicken, increase this to ¾ pint with uncooked chicken

1 Coat the portions of uncooked fowl or chicken in the flour, mixed with the seasoning—ready cooked chicken need not be coated.
2 Peel the onions and peel or scrape the carrots.
3 Put the tomatoes and *bouquet garni* into the blender and switch gradually to high until a thick purée—keep in the goblet until adding rest of ingredients.
4 Fry the chicken in the hot butter until golden (unnecessary with cooked chicken).
5 Lift out of the pan, then toss the onions in the butter.
6 Lift these out and gradually blend in the stock, bring to the boil and cook until thickened—if the cooked chicken has not been fried, then ½ oz. flour should be blended with the butter, after removing the onions.
7 Put 4 onions, the uncooked carrots and the slightly thickened stock into the goblet with the tomato purée, switch gradually to high until blended.
8 Taste the sauce, add extra seasoning if required.
9 Put the chicken joints, whole onions into the saucepan or a casserole, pour on the sauce.
10 Cover the pan or casserole—to cook: Allow 1¾ hours for a boiling fowl in the saucepan or a very moderate oven. Allow 45 minutes for a really young chicken, a little longer if less young. Allow 30 minutes if reheating cooked chicken.

Low calorie ragoût
Omit the flour, use rather less liquid and let the vegetables be the thickening.

Salmis of game
Substitute game for chicken, left, but use partly stock and partly red wine. Cooked chestnuts may be added with the whole onions.

Sour-sweet and ginger pork

cooking time	1 hour
blender speed	medium

you will need for 4 servings:

1¼–1½ lb. pork (cut this from leg or shoulder)	1 oz. fat (optional)—see Stage 2
for the sauce:	3 oz. ginger nut biscuits
2 onions	
2 slices of pineapple or 3–4 oz. pineapple cubes	¼ pint syrup from canned pineapple
1 tablespoon lemon juice or vinegar	¼ pint brown stock, or all pineapple syrup
2 teaspoons sugar or syrup or honey	seasoning
	few drops soy sauce

1 Dice pork, cook gently in a pan until golden on outside. Lift out of pan, put into basin.
2 Chop onions, fry in pork fat, or if insufficient, add fat, heat, then fry onions until nearly tender, do not brown.
3 Put ginger nut biscuits into blender, switch on until fine crumbs. Tip into basin with pork, stir well until blended.
4 Put onions and other ingredients gradually into blender, leave only until finely chopped, NOT a smooth purée.
5 Either return pork and ginger nut crumbs to saucepan or put into casserole.
6 Add sauce, cover pan or casserole, cook steadily for 50 minutes on top of cooker, a little longer in a casserole in centre of a very moderate oven (300–350°F.—Gas Mark 3).
7 Serve with boiled rice or noodles and a green salad.

Variations
Omit ginger nut crumbs, coat pork with 1 oz. flour before frying.
Add a small piece of green pepper (capsicum) to the sauce.
Add a tablespoon mustard or vinegar pickles (cauliflower, gherkins—not onion).

Hungarian steak

cooking time   10—15 minutes
blender speed   high

you will need for 4 servings:

seasoning
4 fillet steaks or portions of rump or sirloin steak
1 clove garlic
2—3 oz. butter
for the sauce:
1 small onion
4—5 medium tomatoes and 3 tablespoons water or use medium can tomatoes

1 green pepper (capsicum)
2 oz. mushrooms (optional)
1—2 teaspoons paprika
good pinch cayenne
salt, pepper
¼ pint soured cream*
to garnish:
paprika

*Instead of soured cream use thin cream and ½ tablespoon lemon juice.

1 Season the steaks lightly and rub on either side with a cut clove garlic.
2 Heat the butter in a large pan and fry the steaks for 2 minutes on either side.
3 Meanwhile prepare the sauce: Skin the onion and tomatoes, remove the core and seeds from the pepper.
4 Put all the ingredients into the blender goblet, switch on gradually to high until a smooth mixture.
5 Pour over the steaks and cook for 6—11 minutes, depending upon how well cooked the meat is preferred.
6 Lift the steaks out of the sauce on to a hot dish, continue to heat the sauce for a few minutes, add the soured cream then pour on top of the steaks.
7 Top with paprika and serve with cooked rice and a green salad.

Beef and bacon galantine

cooking time   1½ hours
mincer speed   medium—or see note

you will need for 4—6 servings:

1 oz. fat
1 medium onion
2 tomatoes
4—6 oz. bacon rashers
1¼ lb. stewing beef or brisket of beef
to coat the tin:
1 oz. butter

3 oz. bread
¼ teaspoon dried sage
seasoning
1 egg

2 oz. crisp breadcrumbs

1 Heat the fat and fry the minced or chopped onion in this, together with the skinned chopped tomatoes.

2 Put the bacon rashers and the beef through the mincer, blend with the onion and tomato mixture.
3 Put the bread through the mincer and add the crumbs to the beef.
4 Blend in the sage, seasoning and egg.
5 Butter a 2 lb. loaf tin or ovenproof dish and coat generously with the crumbs.
6 Put in the mixture, and spread flat on top.
7 Cover with greased, greaseproof paper or foil.
8 Cook for approximately 1¼ hours in the centre of a very moderate oven (300—350°F.—Gas Mark 3).
9 Turn out and serve hot or cold.

Note:
If you have no mincer buy the beef minced by the butcher; make the breadcrumbs in the dry blender, tip out; then put onion and tomatoes into the goblet. Switch on until smooth. Add the bacon (remove rind and bone) and switch on until smooth purée. Simmer in hot fat for 5 minutes then add to minced beef—continue as Stage 4.

Beef galantine
Recipe as above, but omit bacon and tomatoes and use 1½ lb. beef. Blend with 2 eggs or 1 egg and 2 tablespoons stock or milk.

Beef and ham galantine
Recipe as above but use half beef and half ham.

Ham galantine
Recipe as above but use ham in place of beef—it is advisable to include the bacon also. The ham can be cooked but uncooked ham is better.

Sausage meat galantine
Recipe as above but omit the bacon and breadcrumbs and use 8 oz. beef or pork sausage meat.

Chicken and bacon galantine
Use minced raw chicken in place of beef *or* mince dark meat from chicken and dice white meat of chicken.

Creamed chicken galantine

cooking time	$1\frac{1}{2}$ hours
mincer speed	medium

you will need for 6–8 servings:

for the sauce:

2 oz. butter	3 oz. bread
1 oz. flour	a sprig fresh thyme or
$\frac{1}{4}$ pint chicken stock	rosemary
seasoning	2 tablespoons cream
$1\frac{1}{2}$ lb. uncooked chicken	2 eggs

1 Make a chicken sauce with half the butter, all the flour and chicken stock, season well.
2 Put the chicken then the bread through the mincer with the sprig fresh herbs.
3 Blend chicken and bread with the sauce, cream, eggs, and little more seasoning.
4 Press into a buttered 2 lb. loaf tin or ovenproof dish. Cover with buttered greaseproof paper or foil.
5 As this should be a moist texture stand the tin in a dish of cold water.
6 Cook for $1\frac{1}{4}$ hours in the centre of a very moderate oven (300–350°F.—Gas Mark 3).
7 Turn out and serve hot or cold.

Creamed chicken and ham galantine
Use 1 lb. raw chicken and 8 oz. uncooked ham.

Chicken and egg galantine
Use the recipe for creamed chicken galantine. Hard boil 3 eggs, put half the mixture into the tin—add the shelled eggs then cover with the remaining mixture and cook as above.

Onion and potato hot pot

cooking time	$1\frac{1}{2}$–2 hours
use shredder for this	

you will need for 4 servings:

2 lb. neck of lamb—choose	seasoning
best-end-neck, or middle	1–$1\frac{1}{2}$ oz. butter or
neck of lamb	margarine
1 lb. onions	approximately $\frac{1}{4}$ pint stock
$1\frac{1}{2}$ lb. potatoes	or use water and $\frac{1}{2}$ stock
	cube

1 Divide the meat into neat pieces.
2 Put the peeled onions and the peeled potatoes through the shredder of the mixer—keep them separate.
3 Put a layer of meat, seasoning, then onions then potatoes, and fill the casserole like this, seasoning each layer well. Save enough potatoes for the top layer and arrange these in a neat design.
4 The stock can either be poured over at the end or a little added to each layer.
5 Brush the top of the potatoes with the melted butter and cover with a lid.
6 Cook for $1\frac{1}{2}$ hours if using very good quality lamb, as the thinly sliced onions and potatoes will then be cooked; choose the longer time for middle neck of lamb.
7 Cook in the centre of a very moderate to moderate oven (350–375°F.—Gas Mark 4) remove the lid 30 minutes before the end of the cooking time to allow the potatoes to brown.

If using cheaper quality meat then increase the cooking time to 2–$2\frac{1}{2}$ hours and use a very moderate oven (300–350°F.—Gas Mark 3).

Variations

Vegetable hot pot

Omit the meat and arrange thick slices of tomato, thin slices of carrot (also put through the shredder), thin slices of aubergine, in the casserole, and add water or chicken stock.

Hamburgers

cooking time	10 minutes
mincer speed	medium

you will need for 4 servings:

minimum of 1 lb. beef	good pinch mixed herbs
(use good quality beef)	1 egg
1 medium or large onion	**to fry:**
seasoning	little fat

1 Put the beef and onion through the mincer.
2 Add seasoning, herbs, and bind with an egg.
3 Form into about 4 large or 8 smaller flat cakes.
4 Heat the fat in the pan, fry meat steadily on either side. Do not over-cook, for a good Hamburger should be moist and slightly under-cooked in the centre.

Potato burgers

Recipe as above, but put a medium-sized potato through the mincer and add to the meat, etc. The egg can be omitted in this case, as the potato provides quite an amount of liquid.

Shepherd's pie—Method 1

cooking time 35–55 minutes
mixer speed medium
mincer speed medium

you will need for 4 servings:

12 oz.–1 lb. left-over meat
  or poultry
2 medium onions
2 large tomatoes
1–2 oz. dripping or fat
$\frac{1}{2}$–1 oz. flour, see Stage 3
$\frac{1}{2}$–$\frac{3}{4}$ pint brown stock or
  gravy, see Stage 3 or
  use water and stock
  cubes

seasoning
pinch fresh or dried herbs
1–1$\frac{1}{2}$ lb. boiled potatoes
1 oz. butter or margarine
2–3 tablespoons milk

1 Put the meat through the mincer, use the coarse plate.
2 Put the peeled onions through the mincer, skin and chop the tomatoes.
3 Heat the dripping or fat and fry the onions and tomatoes until soft, then gradually blend in the flour (the amount depends upon whether you like a lot of liquid in this particular dish; use $\frac{1}{2}$ oz. with $\frac{1}{2}$ pint liquid or if using a slightly thickened gravy—use 1 oz. if using the $\frac{3}{4}$ pint liquid unless a thick meat mixture is disliked then 'cut down' accordingly). Blend in the liquid, bring to the boil and cook until thickened.
4 Add the meat, do not cook again, season and put in herbs to taste.
5 Put the meat mixture into the pie dish, the potatoes should be well above the meat to brown well, so do not choose too large a dish.
6 Use the whisk to mash the potatoes, see page 41 and blend in the butter and milk, season well.
7 Pipe or pile on to the meat mixture, if they are not piped then mark in an attractive design with a fork.
8 If the meat mixture and potatoes are hot then bake for 35 minutes, just above the centre of a moderate oven (350–375°F.—Gas Mark 4–5). If the food has become cold increase the baking time to 55 minutes, lowering the heat slightly if necessary.
A little extra butter could be put on top of the potatoes to encourage top to brown.

Shepherd's pie—Method 2

1 Use ingredients as above.
2 Instead of mincing the meat, cut into dice.
3 Put the onions and tomatoes with some of the stock into the blender, blend until a thick purée.
4 Heat the fat, stir in the flour and cook for several minutes, add rest of stock and purée and cook until thickened.
5 Continue cooking for about 10 minutes to tenderise the onion, add the meat, etc., then continue as above.

Rissoles

cooking time 25 minutes
mincer speed medium

you will need for 4 servings:

12 oz. cooked meat
2 oz. bread
1 medium onion
2 tomatoes (optional)
either small bunch mixed
  fresh herbs or good pinch
  dried herbs

2 oz. fat or margarine
1 oz. flour
$\frac{1}{4}$ pint brown stock

to coat:
1 egg

2 oz. crisp breadcrumbs
  (raspings)

to fry:
fat or dripping

1 Put the meat through the mincer—use a fine or coarse plate according to personal taste.
2 Put the bread through the mincer, then the onion. The fresh herbs may be minced or chopped.
3 Heat the fat and toss the onion in this until tender. Add tomatoes, peeled and chopped, stir in the flour, cook for several minutes then gradually blend in the stock.
4 Bring to the boil and cook until a thick binding sauce (panada).
5 Stir in the meat, breadcrumbs, and herbs.
6 Allow the mixture to cool then form into 4 or 8 small rounds or ovals.
7 Coat in beaten egg and the crumbs.
8 Fry until crisp and golden brown.

Variation
Creamed chicken rissoles
Use chicken not meat, and instead of brown stock use half milk and half thin cream. Flavour with a little grated lemon rind.

Meat and poultry dishes that are new

1 **Chicken in asparagus sauce:** Grilled or fried or roasted chicken can be topped by a 2 minute sauce . . . tip a medium can of cream of asparagus soup into the blender goblet, add cayenne pepper, 2–3 tablespoons thick cream (or cream cheese). Switch gradually to high then warm and serve with the chicken.

2 **Chicken in sauce provençal:** Grilled or fried chicken or jointed roasted chicken should be heated in this sauce for a short time . . . tip a medium can of tomatoes (or tomato soup) into the blender goblet with 1 skinned clove garlic, 2 tiny shallots or onions. Switch on until blended, season very well. Put into a pan with a good knob of butter and the chicken and heat.

3 **Veal and paprika cream:** Fry the slices of veal in hot butter, put on to a hot dish. Blend $\frac{1}{2}$ pint thin cream with the butter in the pan, tip into the warmed blender goblet with $\frac{1}{2}$–1 tablespoon paprika and 3 oz. cream cheese. Switch on until blended, add 1–2 teaspoons capers. Heat gently, serve on veal. Garnish with paprika and chopped dill or parsley.

Ham mousse with brandy

cooking time	few minutes
blender speed	low
or mincer speed	medium
mixer speed	high

you will need for 6 servings:

1 lb. cooked lean ham	2 eggs
$\frac{3}{4}$ pint aspic jelly	$\frac{1}{4}$ pint thick cream
$\frac{1}{4}$ oz. powder gelatine	salt, pepper, cayenne
$\frac{1}{4}$ pint mayonnaise or	pepper, paprika
Hollandaise sauce	2 tablespoons brandy
2 medium tomatoes	

1 The ham may either be put into the blender for a very smooth mixture or through the coarse or fine plates of the mincer.
If using the blender add about $\frac{1}{4}$ pint aspic jelly to make sure no meat is wasted round the blades in the goblet.

2 Tip the ham into a large bowl.
3 Dissolve the powder gelatine in the very hot aspic jelly, allow this to become cold, but not set.
4 Put the mayonnaise or Hollandaise sauce into the goblet with the skinned tomatoes, emulsify on low speed until blended.
5 Blend with the whisked egg yolks, cool aspic jelly, ham, the cream (whisked with the mixer until it holds its shape), the seasonings and brandy.
6 Allow the mixture to stand in a cool place until it begins to stiffen slightly.
7 Fold in the whisked egg whites, either spoon into a lightly oiled mould or individual moulds or spoon into shallow dishes.
8 When set serve with salad and mayonnaise, or remoulade sauce (see page 48).

Variation
Instead of aspic jelly use really good stock and $\frac{3}{4}$ oz. powder gelatine, add finely grated lemon rind to flavour.
Add diced gherkins and/or truffles at stage 5.
Use approximately 10 oz. cooked ham, proceed to stage 6, then add 8 oz. diced chicken or turkey breast and then the egg whites. The chicken breast can be marinaded in the brandy or choose sherry if preferred.

Lamb with apricot sauce

cooking time	50 minutes
blender speed	low then high

you will need for 4 servings:

4 fillets of lamb, i.e. thin	4 oz. dried apricots
slices cut from the top	(soaked for some hours
of the leg	in cold water to cover) or
2 oz. butter	medium can of apricots
2 medium onions	good pinch cinnamon
1 clove garlic (optional)	2 medium carrots
	seasoning

1 Fry the meat in the hot butter until golden on either side, then lift out of the pan.
2 Chop the onions and toss in the butter, with the crushed clove garlic.
3 Replace the meat in the pan, add the apricots and the water in which the fruit was soaked (this should be approximately $\frac{3}{4}$ pint). If using canned apricots add the syrup from the can and a squeeze lemon juice to minimise the sweet flavour.
4 Add the cinnamon, the sliced carrots and a generous amount of seasoning.
5 Cover the pan and simmer steadily for 35–40 minutes.
6 Lift the meat from the sauce, put on to a hot dish, then put the sauce into the warmed goblet. Switch gradually to high until a smooth sauce.
7 Pour over the lamb—if wished a few apricot halves may be kept whole and used as garnish.

Stuffings

A good stuffing makes meat, fish, poultry and vegetable dishes more satisfying and interesting and with the help of the blender these may be prepared in an almost unbelievably short time. Detailed information about the order of putting the ingredients into the goblet is given under the individual recipes but remember:

a Make sure the goblet is dry before adding the bread, etc.
b Do not put too much food in at one time.
c The moment the blades cease to revolve it is safe to assume that the goblet is filled to maximum capacity *for that particular mixture*—do not waste time trying to pack more food in the goblet, tip the prepared stuffing into a bowl and process more of the ingredients.
d It may be possible to add extra bread, parsley, etc., as the motor is running, in rather the same way as the oil is added in a mayonnaise. This is particularly suitable if using fresh bread in a stuffing.
e Use your own stuffing recipe as well as those given but remember you extract all the flavour from the parsley and other herbs, whereas when you chop these on a board some of the juice is wasted. This means you may need to use a little less parsley to keep the balance of flavour.

Warning: Do not try to remove ingredients with a sharp knife, you could damage the blades in the goblet as well as the knife. Switch OFF, then tip goblet over a bowl, if some ingredients remain in the goblet, help these out using the special spatula if provided or with a flat-bladed knife.

NEVER use any knife, spatula, etc., while the machine is in operation.

See comments about filling goblet under soups, page 15.

Veal stuffing

cooking time	as particular recipe being used
blender speed	low then high

you will need for 4 servings:

enough parsley to give up to 1 tablespoon when chopped	4 oz. bread (weight with crusts removed)
fresh herbs to give up to $\frac{1}{2}$ teaspoon when chopped, or use $\frac{1}{4}$ teaspoon dried herbs	few strips lemon peel
	2 oz. suet or melted margarine or butter
	1 egg
	seasoning

1 Wash and dry the parsley and fresh herbs; while they can be used when damp, this is inclined to prevent the blades working as well, as the damp parsley becomes slightly clogged with the bread.
2 Cut or break the bread into convenient sized pieces.
3 Put a very little bread and parsley and herbs into the dry blender goblet, together with pieces of lemon rind and suet (not melted fat).
4 Switch to low and then either remove the cap from the lid or tilt the lid itself so that none of

the ingredients will be lost and gradually 'feed' bread and parsley into the goblet.

5 The moment you find the mixture does not move, switch off—remove from the goblet or you may find it worthwhile switching momentarily to high speed which may 'dislodge' the crumb and herb mixture from the goblet, so you may continue adding a little more.

6 When the first amount of bread, etc., is smooth, tip out and continue with more bread, etc.

7 Do not add the melted margarine and egg to the mixture in the goblet, this must be added to the crumbs in a basin. Put all the crumbs, etc., into a basin and bind with egg and add seasoning to taste.

Note the remarks on page 32 about quantity of herbs to add; this naturally depends upon personal taste, but the difference in strength of flavour from parsley, etc., is very marked.

Note remarks under bread sauce, page 38, if using very fresh bread.

Veal stuffing is served with: veal, chicken, turkey, etc.

Giblet stuffing

Cook the giblets and when tender, add the liver (or liver, heart and meat from the neck, etc.) to the bread in the veal stuffing. It is advisable to do this with the last batch or two batches of bread since the rather moist meat is inclined to make the goblet sticky.

The parsley may be omitted if wished. Serve with poultry.

Liver stuffing

Cook 2–3 oz. calves' or lambs' liver or the liver from the poultry in 1 oz. butter or chicken fat. Add to veal stuffing ingredients in the blender. Serve with veal, poultry. This is also very delicious with lamb.

Mushroom stuffing

cooking time   as particular recipe used
blender speed   medium

you will need for 4 servings:

3 oz. bread (wholemeal bread is very good in this recipe)	1 small onion
	4 oz. mushrooms or mushroom stalks
1 tablespoon chopped parsley	2 oz. butter or margarine seasoning

1 Put the bread and parsley into the dry blender goblet, switch on until fairly coarsely chopped.

2 Tip into a bowl, then add the onion and well-dried mushrooms, switch on until finely chopped, mix with the bread and the remainder of the ingredients (melting the butter or margarine).

To serve with veal, lamb or poultry, or fish.

Variations

Add 3–4 oz. finely chopped cooked ham or crisply fried bacon at stage 2.
Add 4–6 oz. diced cucumber at stage 2.

Sage and onion stuffing

cooking time   as particular recipe being used
blender speed   low then high

you will need for 4 servings:

2 large onions (peeled)	1 oz. suet or melted butter
2 oz. breadcrumbs (weight with crusts removed)	good pinch salt and pepper
1 teaspoon dried sage or fresh sage to give 2 teaspoons when mixed with bread	

1 Put the onions into a saucepan, adding $\frac{1}{2}$ pint water.

2 Simmer steadily for about 20 minutes when the onions will be partly cooked.

3 Remove from water on to chopping board and chop into small pieces.

4 Emulsify the bread and the sage as in veal stuffing.

5 Mix with the onions adding the suet or butter, seasoning and enough onion stock to give a moist texture.

6 Serve with duck, pork, goose or many savoury dishes.

Celery and raisin stuffing

cooking time   as particular recipe used
mincer or shredder speed   medium

you will need for 4 servings:

small head of celery (discard the tough outer stalks)	$\frac{1}{2}$ teaspoon chopped lemon thyme
1 large onion	1 lemon, seasoning
2 oz. butter or margarine	4 tablespoons stock
1 teaspoon chopped parsley	6 oz. seedless raisins

1 Put the celery and the celery leaves through a coarse mincer or through the vegetable shredder.
2 Mince or shred the onion.
3 Toss together in the hot butter.
4 Add the herbs, these may also be put through the mincer or put into the blender goblet.
5 Add the grated lemon rind and plenty of seasoning.
6 Squeeze the juice from the lemon, heat with the stock and pour over the raisins—this makes them 'plump up'. Add to the celery, etc. Excellent with most poultry or with pork.

Chestnut stuffing

cooking time   as particular recipe being used
blender speed   low then high

you will need for 4 servings:

1 lb. chestnuts   2 oz. breadcrumbs
8 oz. chopped cooked   ¾–1 pint ham or chicken
  ham (optional)   stock
little milk   2 oz. butter

1 Split the chestnuts and boil for about 10 minutes in water.
2 Remove the skins, and simmer the nuts in stock until very tender.
3 Lift the chestnuts out of the stock.
4 Put the ingredients into the blender in the same way as veal stuffing.
5 This stuffing can be varied by adding chopped onion, mixed herbs or parsley, but do not use too strong flavours to obscure the delicious chestnut taste.
This stuffing is served with chicken, turkey; for a large turkey you will need about twice to three times the quantity.

Walnut stuffing

cooking time   as particular recipe used
blender speed   medium

you will need for 4 servings:

3 oz. soft bread (weight   3 oz. seedless raisins
  without crusts)   seasoning
4 oz. walnuts, shelled   pinch chopped or dried
1 lemon   rosemary
1–2 oz. preserved or   2 tablespoons oil
  stem ginger

1 Put the bread into the blender goblet on medium speed, to give a fairly coarse crumb.
2 Repeat with the walnuts, add tiny strips of lemon rind and leave these until very fine.
3 Chop the ginger, squeeze the juice from the lemon.
4 Mix all the ingredients together. Serve with poultry or veal—the amount given allows a generous portion.

Mixed nut stuffing
Use 1 oz. pistachio nuts, 1 oz. pine nuts, 2 oz. walnuts.

Rice nut stuffing
Use 3 oz. cooked long grain rice instead of breadcrumbs.

To cook stuffings

When stuffing is put in with the meat or poultry, this should be weighed after stuffing, and the cooking time calculated accordingly.
In some cases, however, the stuffing will be cooked in a separate dish and it should be given from 30 to 40 minutes in a moderately hot oven (375–400°F.—Gas Mark 5).

Making sauces

If by chance you have made a sauce and it looks lumpy, do not worry, put it into the blender and in a few minutes the sauce will be perfectly smooth; in fact sauces put into the blender and left for about 30 seconds on full speed have an almost unbelievable smoothness. It does tend to make sauces a little less stiff in consistency. Mint sauce is made in a matter of seconds. See the recipe, page 36.
Mayonnaise and similar sauces are highly successful and quickly made in a blender. Make sure the egg yolks and oil are at room temperature.
A perfect sauce depends upon careful weighing of ingredients, on cooking the right way, but above all else, on its smooth texture. The

blender will help you achieve this with the minimum of trouble.

Warning: Read the comments about filling goblet, etc., under soups, page 15.

White sauce 1

cooking time   5—8 minutes
blender speed   high

you will need for 4 servings:

sauce
  (coating consistency) $\frac{1}{2}$ pint milk
1 oz. butter or margarine   salt and pepper
1 oz. flour

1 Heat the butter gently, remove from the heat and stir in the flour.
2 Return to the heat and cook gently for a few minutes, so that the 'roux', as the butter and flour mixture is called, does not brown.
3 Again remove the pan from the heat and gradually blend in the cold milk.
4 Bring to the boil and cook, stirring with a wooden spoon until smooth.
5 Season well. Pour the sauce into the warmed blender goblet.
6 Switch gradually to high. Leave on high until the sauce is very smooth.
7 Either return to the pan and reheat or use at once.

Panada.
Use ingredients as above but only $\frac{1}{4}$ pint milk.

White sauce 2

cooking time   5—8 minutes
blender speed   high

you will need for 4 servings:

Ingredients as above, but blend the flour and milk in the blender goblet. Tip into the pan with the butter and seasoning, bring to the boil and cook until smooth, stirring well. Return to the blender goblet as above.

Cheese sauce

cooking time   5—8 minutes
blender speed   high

you will need for 4 servings:

3 oz. Cheddar or other   Ingredients as white sauce
  cooking cheese

1 Put the cheese into the blender goblet as described on page 10 until fine. Tip out.
2 Make the white sauce as given on the left. When thick add the cheese and cook until just melted.
3 A cheese sauce can be seasoned with a generous amount of mustard.
Never emulsify the cheese with the milk otherwise the cheese sauce will be spoiled for the cheese will over-cook and curdle.

Parsley sauce

cooking time   8 minutes
blender speed   high

you will need for 4 servings:

Ingredients as white   Approximately 1 table-
  sauce   spoon of parsley

There are 3 ways of making a parsley sauce.
a If you wish the parsley to look rather a bright green and be firm, make the white sauce in the usual way, add the parsley when the sauce has thickened and emulsify in the goblet.
b Put the parsley into the dry blender goblet and switch on until finely 'chopped'. Make the sauce in the usual way and add the parsley at the end. This may be returned to the blender if wished.
c This method gives a more bland flavour to the sauce as the parsley is cooked for a longer period. Put the milk and parsley into the blender goblet. Switch on until the parsley is very fine.
Make the white sauce in the usual way with the parsley flavoured milk.

8 ways to add variety to a white sauce

Anchovy sauce

Put approximately 6 anchovy fillets into the blender goblet with the white sauce. Switch on until emulsified.

Excellent with fish or to serve over hard-boiled eggs.

Caper sauce

Although many people like whole capers in the sauce, some people dislike this and the flavour of caper sauce can be given by adding two tea-spoons of capers, plus a little vinegar from the jar to the white sauce and emulsifying until smooth. If serving caper sauce with lamb, use half milk and half stock.

Dill sauce

Use dill in place of parsley.
Excellent with fish.

Fennel sauce

As parsley sauce using sprigs of fennel leaves. Ideal with fish.

Hard-boiled egg sauce

Put the white sauce into the warmed blender goblet. Add two hard-boiled eggs, plus a sprig of parsley if wished. Switch on until as fine as desired.

Horseradish sauce

Put the white sauce into the warmed blender goblet. Add 1–2 tablespoons of horseradish cut into small pieces, 1 tablespoon of cream and $\frac{1}{2}$–1 tablespoon lemon juice or vinegar, plus a pinch of sugar. Switch on until emulsified. Try not to reheat this sauce or it might curdle.

Mushroom sauce

Fry 2–4 oz. mushrooms in 1 oz. butter. Add to white sauce in warmed blender goblet and switch on until as fine as required.

Creamy tomato sauce

Put the very hot white sauce into the warmed blender goblet. Add either 2 skinned de-seeded, fresh tomatoes or 1–2 tablespoons concentrated tomato purée. Switch on until emulsified.

It is better not to reheat this sauce as it might curdle.

Taste and season very well.

Mint sauce

blender speed	high

you will need for 4 servings:

2–3 tablespoons mint leaves	approximately 3 table-spoons white wine or
1 oz. sugar	brown malt vinegar

1 Put the mint leaves into the blender goblet with the other ingredients.
2 Switch on until the mint is chopped. This tends to give a rather finely chopped mint sauce.
   If a coarser mint sauce is required, put the sugar and vinegar into the blender goblet. Switch on to a fairly low speed and add the mint leaves gradually. In this way, they are less finely chopped.

Note:

A mint sauce looks very cloudy when made in a blender, so allow 10–15 minutes for it to stand and clear.

Brown sauce

cooking time	15–20 minutes
blender speed	high

you will need for 4 servings:

sauce (coating consistency)	$\frac{1}{2}$ pint brown stock or water and a stock cube
1–2 oz. dripping or fat	salt, pepper and a pinch mustard
1 onion	
1 carrot	
1 oz. flour	

panada
(binding consistency)
as above, but use $\frac{1}{4}$ pint stock only

To add to casseroles, etc., as above, but use $\frac{1}{2}$–$\frac{3}{4}$ pint stock depending upon the recipe.
1 Heat the dripping or fat and fry the finely chopped onion and carrot for 5 minutes.
2 Stir in flour and cook for 2–3 minutes.

3 Gradually blend in the stock and seasoning.

4 Bring to the boil, stirring all the time with a wooden spoon until smooth.

5 Season well although the amount of seasoning will depend upon the particular dish for which this is being used.

6 Pour the sauce into the warmed blender goblet. Switch gradually to high. Leave on high until the sauce is very smooth.

7 Either return to the pan and reheat or use at once.

Espagnole sauce
(Spanish sauce)

Use 2 oz. fat and fry 1–2 tomatoes, 1 onion, 1 carrot, 2 mushrooms and a small piece of green pepper (capsicum) in the fat. Proceed as brown sauce but flavour with a little sherry and add a *bouquet garni* to the stock when making the sauce.

Excellent in many meat or poultry casserole dishes.

Quick Bigarade sauce
(Orange sauce)

Make the brown sauce or the Espagnole sauce, but put pieces of orange rind into the liquid when cooking and use partly stock and partly orange juice, according to personal taste. After the sauce has been put into the blender add more small pieces of orange rind.

This sauce is excellent with duck, goose, or pork. A little port wine may be added to flavour if wished.

Velvet curry sauce

cooking time	$1\frac{1}{4}$ hours
blender speed	high

you will need for 4 servings:

1 medium sized onion	1 dessertspoon chutney
1 cooking apple, cored	1 tablespoon desiccated
1 oz. butter	coconut
1 level tablespoon curry	1 dessertspoon sultanas
powder	1 teaspoon lemon juice
1 teaspoon curry paste	seasoning
1 level tablespoon	1–2 tablespoons milk or
cornflour	cream*
$\frac{1}{2}$ pint stock or water	

*This can be omitted with meat curries.

1 Peel and chop the onion and apple.

2 Fry in the hot butter.

3 Add curry powder, paste and cornflour.

4 Stir until blended, cook a few minutes and then stir in stock. Bring to boil, stirring all the time.

5 Add chutney, coconut and sultanas.

6 Cover and simmer for at least 1 hour.

7 Stir in the lemon juice, add seasoning and the milk or cream.

8 Pour into the warmed blender goblet. Switch to high very gradually and leave until smooth.

9 This particular curry sauce is then returned to the pan with the pieces of cooked meat, chicken, shell fish or hard-boiled eggs and reheated or cooked for the required time.

Apple sauce

cooking time	10–15 minutes
blender speed	high

you will need for 4–6 servings:

1 lb. apples	1 oz. butter or margarine
2 oz. sugar	water—see method

1 Peel and core apples and slice.

2 Put into saucepan with the sugar, butter and little water.

3 The amount of water depends on the type of apple but a blender tends to give a slightly softer texture so be sparing with this.

4 Simmer until the apples are tender—there is no need to make this into a smooth purée.

5 Pour into the warmed blender goblet.

6 Switch gradually to high. Take particular care to see the lid is firmly in position and the goblet not over-filled.

7 Leave until smooth.

Reheat if wished.

Cranberry sauce

cooking time	10–15 minutes
blender speed	high

you will need for 4–6 servings:

8–12 oz. cranberries	2–3 oz. sugar
$\frac{1}{4}$ pint water	knob of butter

Method as apple sauce.

Tomato sauce 1

cooking time	15 minutes
blender speed	low then high

you will need for 4 servings:

1 oz. butter or bacon fat	½ pint water
½ apple	1 small can tomato purée
½ onion	1 beef stock cube (optional)
2 teaspoons cornflour	salt, pepper

1 Heat the butter or fat.
2 Peel and cut the apple and onion into fairly small pieces, and fry for a few minutes.
3 Blend cornflour with water and stir, with the tomato purée, into the pan.
4 Add stock cube and season to taste.
5 Bring sauce to the boil and cook until thickened.
6 Pour into the warmed blender goblet, switch on until smooth.

Tomato sauce 2

cooking time	25 minutes
blender speed	low then high

you will need for 4 servings:

1 oz. butter or bacon fat	seasoning, including celery
2 rashers bacon	salt, cayenne or paprika
1 onion	pepper
1 lb. tomatoes	2 teaspoons cornflour
¾ pint water or white stock	pinch brown sugar

1 Heat the butter or bacon fat.
2 Chop the bacon into small pieces and peel and chop onion.
3 Toss in the butter or fat (add bacon rinds if wished).
4 Skin the tomatoes and de-seed if you want a very smooth tomato sauce.
5 Add to the bacon and onion with ½ pint of the water, and seasoning.
6 Simmer until tomatoes are soft.
7 Blend the cornflour with the remaining water.
8 Stir into the purée and cook until thickened.
9 Remove bacon rinds and spoon or pour ingredients into warmed blender goblet.
10 Switch to low then gradually to high until smooth.
11 Taste and add more seasoning and sugar.
12 Reheat if wished.

Bread sauce

cooking time	10 minutes
blender speed	low

you will need for 4 servings:

1 small onion	seasoning
2 or 3 cloves, if liked	4 oz. bread (weight when
½ pint milk	crusts removed)
1–2 oz. butter or margarine	

1 Peel the onion, and stick cloves into it if wished.
2 Put with milk and butter or margarine in a pan, slowly bring to boil, season well.
3 Remove from the heat, add crumbs and leave in a warm place for as longs as possible.
4 To make these crumbs, add bread gradually to the dry blender goblet—with machine in operation. Use low speed for moderately stale bread. If using fresh bread, use a high speed and do not put any bread into the goblet until you have switched on. Add this gradually with the cap removed from the lid or the lid tilted slightly.
5 Just before the meal is ready, heat the sauce gently, remove onion before serving.

Kefta sauce

This Moroccan sauce is excellent to serve with kebabs and rice or with grilled or fried meats.

cooking time	see Stage 2
blender speed	low then high

you will need for 4–5 servings:

4 large tomatoes	pinch powdered ginger
1 medium onion (2–3	parsley to give 1 table-
spring onions give a	spoon when chopped
milder flavour)	mint to give 2 teaspoons
1–2 cloves garlic	when chopped
2–3 tablespoons olive oil	water, see Stage 1
(may be reduced)	seasoning
good pinch cayenne pepper	

1 Put all ingredients into the blender, adding enough water to give a thick purée if to serve cold; if intending to have this sauce hot, then you need a slightly thinner purée.
2 Serve hot or cold—if serving hot, simmer until all the vegetables are tender and the mixture is thick again—approximately 20 minutes.

If serving cold, make quite certain the ingredients are well blended.

Hollandaise sauce

cooking time   about 10 minutes
mixer speed   low

you will need for 4–5 servings:

2 egg yolks
1–2 tablespoons lemon
   juice or vinegar (use
   white, malt or wine
   vinegar or mix tarragon
   and ordinary vinegar)
seasoning—include pinch
   cayenne pepper and
   pinch mustard (optional)
2–4 oz. butter

Note:

This is made by continuously whisking as the eggs thicken over heat, so a portable whisk is ideal for this.

1 Put the egg yolks, lemon juice or vinegar and seasoning into the basin, stand this securely over a bowl of hot water. DO NOT ALLOW the water to boil.
2 Whisk until light, fluffy looking and thick.
3 If the butter is very hard soften this, but do not allow to become 'oily'.
4 Whisk the butter in very gradually—if added too quickly it becomes a curdled mixture or a very 'oily' one. Use the smaller quantity of butter to serve with vegetables, the larger for salmon or other fish.

Béarnaise sauce

This is made as Hollandaise sauce, but a chopped shallot, few chopped herbs and extra pepper (use peppercorns) are infused with the vinegar—and tarragon is generally the choice of vinegar. Strain vinegar. Serve with steak.

Mousseline sauce

As Hollandaise sauce, but use only 1 oz. butter, remove from the heat, blend in 2 tablespoons thick cream and a little grated nutmeg. Serve with vegetables or fish.

Barbecue sauce

blender speed   high

you will need for 4 servings:

3 spring onions
4 tomatoes
2 tablespoons stock or
   water
1 tablespoon Worcester-
   shire sauce
1 tablespoon vinegar
2 tablespoons sweet
   chutney
2 tablespoons oil
pinch curry powder
   seasoning
2 teaspoons brown sugar

1 Put all the ingredients into the blender.
2 Switch on until smoothly blended.
Brush chicken, chops, etc., with this when cooking over a barbecue.

Relishes

A relish can take the place of a stuffing. It is cooked separately or served cold. The same advice about choice of relish applies as with stuffing—choose flavours that do not conflict with the taste of the meat, fish or poultry.

Sanfayna

This adaptation from a Spanish recipe makes a delicious relish for vegetable and meat dishes.

cooking time   20 minutes
blender speed   medium

you will need for 4–5 servings:

1 green pepper (capsicum)
1 red pepper
1 large onion
4 large tomatoes
1–2 small courgettes
2 cloves garlic
3 tablespoons olive oil
seasoning

1 Chop the vegetables coarsely and crush the garlic.
2 Fry steadily in the oil until fairly soft—do not overcook.
3 Put into the blender goblet, warming this if the vegetables are put in very hot.
4 Switch on until a fairly smooth mixture.
5 Tip out and season highly.
Serve hot or cold.

Variation

Blend when cold with mayonnaise and serve with cold meat.

Spiced prunes

cooking time   1 hour
blender speed   low then high

you will need for 6 servings:

¾ pint water	3 oz. brown sugar
1 lemon	2 tablespoons vinegar
1 apple (fairly sweet)	½–1 teaspoon allspice
2 peppercorns	12 oz. prunes

1 Put the water, the thinly pared lemon rind, peeled chopped apple and the other ingredients except prunes into the blender goblet.
2 Switch gradually to high until smoothly blended.
3 Pour over prunes and leave soaking overnight.
4 Simmer gently until the prunes are tender. Serve with pork, duck, goose (either hot or cold).

Lemon pepper relish

cooking time   20 minutes
mincer or shredder speed   medium

you will need for 4–5 servings:

2 medium green peppers	1 teaspoon cinnamon
2 lemons	1 oz. butter
2 oz. brown sugar	1 tablespoon water

1 Put the pulp of the peppers through the mincer or shredder, discarding core and seeds.
2 Put the finely pared lemon rind through at the same time.
3 Squeeze out the lemon juice.

4 Put all the ingredients into a pan and simmer steadily until soft and thick. Cool or serve hot. Serve with cold meats.

Date relish

blender speed   medium

you will need for 4–5 servings:

2 tablespoons boiling water	pinch powdered ginger
2 tablespoons vinegar	pinch powdered cinnamon
1 shallot or tiny onion	8 oz. stoned dates

1 Put the water, vinegar, onion, ginger and cinnamon into the blender goblet, switch on until blended.
2 Pour over the halved dates, stand for several hours.
Serve with cold meat.

Mint relish

blender speed   medium then high

you will need for 4–5 servings:

½ cucumber	seasoning
large bunch mint	sugar to taste
2–3 tablespoons vinegar	

1 Peel the cucumber, dice; remove leaves from the sprigs of mint.
2 Put into blender goblet with vinegar and switch on until blended.
3 Add seasoning and sugar to taste.
Serve with hot or cold lamb.

Vegetable cookery

One of the interesting facts about cooking vegetables is that in most cases the quicker they are cooked the better the flavour. This means that if vegetables are cut into small pieces they tend to retain more flavour—and perhaps even more important—more vitamins. In the following recipes the mincer or slicer

and shredder of a mixer is invaluable, but in some cases the recipes make use of the whisk and/or blender.

To speed the cooking of vegetables
Put the skinned or peeled vegetables through the coarse mincer if you are in a great hurry or

through the slicer. This means they cook in record time. Be careful, however, they do not become over-cooked; and because they are so finely chopped, the absolute minimum of water should be used in cooking.

Mashing vegetables

If you have a small portable mixer then lower this into pan of drained, cooked vegetables—use a low speed to begin with until the larger lumps are broken down (or break these with a fork first) then as the mixture becomes softer increase the speed. Add any butter, milk, etc., and whisk until thoroughly blended. With the larger mixtures tip the well drained vegetables into the warmed mixing bowl, and proceed as above. If you only have the blender and no mixer then the vegetables can be put into the warmed blender goblet—*do not over-fill*. In order to save the mixture clogging the blades it is a good idea to put the warmed milk into the goblet BEFORE the vegetables. Where you have a choice of whisk or blender remember the whisk gives a lighter more 'fluffy' texture—the blender a very smooth purée. Most usual vegetables to purée: potatoes, carrots, swedes, turnips, etc.

Recipes using mashed vegetables
Potatoes
Duchesse potatoes

Blend 2 oz. margarine into each 1 lb. mashed potatoes, with the yolks of 1–2 eggs and seasoning. Omit the milk. This is used for piping as a border round dishes or to pipe into rose shapes, brown in the oven and serve as a separate vegetable.

Potato cakes

Mash the potatoes, but do not add more than 1 oz. margarine and 2 tablespoons milk to each 1 lb. cooked potatoes. Blend 1–2 oz. self-raising flour with the potato mixture, the amount will vary according to the softness of the vegetable, season well. Remove from the bowl on to a floured board. Press out (or roll with floured rolling pin) to about ½ inch thick,

cut into rounds or triangles and put on to a greased baking sheet and bake for approximately 15 minutes in a hot oven (425–450°F.—Gas Mark 7–8).
If preferred fry in a little hot fat. Serve with cooked meat, bacon, eggs, etc.

Sweet potato cakes

The method of making these is as above but use 8 oz. potatoes (weight when cooked) and 1 oz. margarine, 2 tablespoons milk. Add 8 oz. self-raising flour, 2 oz. sugar, 2 oz. dried fruit. Blend well and mix with 1 egg or part of an egg. Shape and bake as for savoury potato cakes.

Potato croquettes

Mash the potatoes with margarine only, season well. If the vegetable mixture seems a little soft to handle blend in a small amount of flour, but this should not be necessary. Form into finger shapes, then coat in seasoned flour, then beaten egg and crisp breadcrumbs.
Heat a pan of deep fat or oil, test carefully, for if too hot then the croquettes will break during cooking, if too cool then the outside will be greasy. If using fat, a cube of day-old bread should brown within 1 minute, if using oil then it should brown within ½ minute. Put the croquettes into the frying basket, lower into the fat or oil and fry until crisp and golden brown. Drain on absorbent paper.

Jacket potato soufflé

Bake 4 large potatoes in their jackets—allow approximately 1½ hours in the centre of a moderate oven (375°F.—Gas Mark 4–5). Remove from the oven, split through the centre (hold with a clean cloth as they are very hot, and it is easier to cream the pulp while hot). Spoon the pulp into a hot bowl, add 1 oz. butter, seasoning, 2 egg yolks and cream until smooth. Pile back into the potato cases (or use 4 individual soufflé dishes if preferred). Whisk the egg whites until very stiff, add seasoning and 2 oz. finely grated Parmesan or Cheddar cheese, pile over the hot pulp and set for 15 minutes in a moderate oven (375°F.—Gas Mark 4–5).

Potato cheese soufflé

cooking time	45 minutes
mixer speed	low then high

you will need for 4 servings:

1 lb. potatoes (weight before peeling)	3 eggs
	6 tablespoons milk
seasoning	3–4 oz. grated Cheddar
2 oz. butter	cheese

1 Peel and cook the potatoes in well seasoned water until quite soft, strain.
2 Either mash in the saucepan or transfer to warmed mixing bowl, mash and return to the pan, then wash up mixer bowl.
3 Whisk the butter into the hot potato mixture, then add the egg yolks, and the milk—the amount given should be correct but if the potatoes become a little soft in cooking you may need a little less, the mixture should be fairly soft at this stage.
4 Wash the whisk, stir in cheese with spoon.
5 Whisk the egg whites until very stiff, fold into the potato mixture with any seasoning desired, put into a 7-inch soufflé or ovenproof dish and bake in a moderately hot oven (400°F.—Gas Mark 5–6) until golden and firm.

Tomato potato soufflé

Ingredients as above but put a layer of sliced well-seasoned tomatoes in the soufflé dish, heat for 10 minutes in the oven, then add the potato mixture.

Carrots

Carrot and cheese soufflé

Use mashed carrots instead of potatoes or use half potatoes and half carrots. Add a little grated nutmeg as well as cheese to the mixture.

Carrot cheese bake

Cook and mash carrots then arrange a layer in a pie dish, top with sliced cheese and sliced tomatoes, season these well. Continue filling the dish, ending the layers with one of carrot. Top with soft breadcrumbs and grated cheese, together with a few knobs of butter. Bake for approximatcly 30 minutes in the centre of a moderately hot oven (400°F.—Gas Mark 6). Excellent by itself or with grilled bacon or sausages.

Aubergines

Aubergine purée

Aubergines or egg plants make an excellent purée often served as a type of pâté, but equally good as a vegetable.

Split the aubergines across the centre, 'score' the skin with a knife, sprinkle lightly with salt, and allow to stand for about 20 minutes—this takes away the somewhat bitter taste of this vegetable.

To serve as a vegetable:
Brush with oil and bake for approximately 1 hour in a very moderate oven (300–350°F.—Gas Mark 3) until soft. Tip the hot purée (not the skin) into a hot bowl and cream with the whisk, adding a knob of butter, seasoning and a little garlic salt, or put into the warmed blender goblet and emulsify

To serve as a pâté:
Cook more slowly until completely black in colour. Remove the skin if wished, although this often becomes so soft that it can be emulsified. Put ½ tablespoon oil (to 1 large aubergine), 1–2 teaspoons lemon juice, 1 clove garlic into the blender. Add the aubergine and emulsify at low speed until a smooth purée. Do this while vegetable is hot as it is less stiff and easier to blend.

Slicing vegetables

There are many recipes where sliced vegetables are required, follow directions for using the slicer, and the speed of operation recommended.

Recipes for sliced vegetables

Aubergines or egg plant:

Fried: Put the washed, dried aubergines through the slicer. Coat the thin slices with seasoned flour, and fry until crisp and brown in hot shallow or deep oil or fat—there is no need to allow these to stand before cooking, as suggested above, because the amount of skin on each slice is very little. Serve instead of fried potatoes with meat or fish.

Courgettes (or zucchini) . . . baby marrow:

Proceed as for aubergines, do not peel or remove the seeds. Either coat in flour or in batter and fry. Excellent with meat and fish dishes.

Cabbage (and the green vegetables):

Put through the slicer to give really thin strips, these will cook in a far shorter time than when hand shredded.

To make a change toss the shredded cabbage in hot butter, together with a shredded onion. Add just enough hot stock to moisten, season lightly and cook until just tender— approximately 5–8 minutes.

Carrots:

Fried carrots are delicious and rarely cooked today, shred the carrots and fry steadily in shallow hot butter or fat, toss in chopped parsley. Serve with meat, fish or cheese dishes.

Cucumber:

This vegetable is most interesting if when cooked it is put through the shredder, remove peel if tough.

To fry: Coat the thin slices in seasoned flour and fry until crisp in shallow or deep hot oil or fat, or fry steadily in hot butter, do not coat. Excellent with fish dishes.

To boil: Simmer steadily until tender, either in boiling salted water or in seasoned white stock. Strain and toss in butter and chopped parsley.

Celery:

To cook this put through the shredder, not slicer, and cook in boiling salted water until soft, drain well, and toss in butter and chopped parsley or coat with cheese sauce.

Leeks:

Shred the leeks and toss the thin slices in hot butter until tender. Season well. Another way to serve these is to cook until just tender, then add several well beaten eggs to the mixture and cook steadily until the eggs are lightly scrambled. Serve on toast as a savoury.

If preferred the cooked leeks may be put into a shallow dish, topped with cheese sauce and grated cheese and breadcrumbs then browned under a hot grill.

Marrow:

As courgettes or cook as follows:

Marrow Provençal:

You need enough marrow to serve 4 people. Peel the marrow unless very young; put through the shredder. Put 2 large onions through the shredder, then slice 3 large tomatoes and crush a clove of garlic. Fry the onions and garlic in 2 tablespoons oil, add the tomatoes and the marrow and simmer gently together. Cover the pan so the mixture does not become too dry, or add a very little stock. Season well. Serve this hot or cold as a main dish or hors d'œuvre. Courgettes or zucchini could be used instead.

Onions:

Put the peeled onions through the shredder, separate into pieces and fry steadily in hot oil or butter or dripping.

Potatoes:

Game chips or game crisps:

Put the peeled potatoes through the shredder, dry well and fry in very hot deep oil or fat until crisp and golden brown. Drain well on absorbent paper. Serve with cooked game or other savoury dishes or as a cocktail savoury.

Devilled crisps:

Toss the shredded potato slices in flour to which is added a good pinch cayenne pepper, curry powder and chilli powder. Fry as game crisps. Excellent as a cocktail savoury.

Lyonnaise potatoes:

Normally in this dish the potatoes are partially cooked, but because they can be shredded so thinly it is possible to cook the dish as follows:

Put equal quantities of peeled potatoes and onions through the slicer. Fry gently in a generous amount of oil, fat or dripping until tender.

43

Potatoes Anna:

Put the potatoes through the shredder. Grease a cake tin or ovenproof round dish with well clarified dripping. Put a layer of potatoes in this, covered with seasoning and brushed with melted butter or dripping. Continue filling the dish like this. Bake for approximately 1–1¼ hours in the centre of a moderate oven (350–375°F.—Gas Mark 4–5) until golden brown and crisp. Turn out of the tin carefully so the shape remains perfect. Serve with meat, fish or poultry dishes.

Potatoes au gratin:

Method as potatoes Anna, but put grated cheese between each layer. Top with grated cheese, fine breadcrumbs and a little melted butter.

Scalloped potatoes:

Put the peeled potatoes through the slicer. Put in layers into a greased pie dish, seasoning each layer well, and adding a little butter or margarine. Cover the potatoes with milk. Bake for approximately 1½ hours in the centre of a very moderate oven (300–350°F.—Gas Mark 3–4) until tender. The milk should have evaporated at the end of this time, but the potatoes should be moist. Top with chopped parsley. Excellent with all meat, fish or poultry dishes—whether hot or cold.

Savoury scalloped potatoes:

Use canned tomato, mushroom, asparagus or cream of chicken soup instead of milk. If the soup is thick dilute it slightly with water or with milk (do not use milk with the tomato soup otherwise the mixture might curdle).
Thinly sliced onions may be put between the layers of potato in scalloped potatoes.

Swedes and turnips:

Can be shredded and used with, or in the same way as potatoes.

Using the shredder or mincer:

All the vegetables above could be shredded or minced instead of being sliced. Naturally the appearance is not as good. In the following recipes, however, a mincer (or shredder) is better.

Vegetable pancakes:

Put 8 oz. vegetables through the mincer or shredder. Use *all* potatoes or carrots or a mixture of vegetables. Put into a bowl, add seasoning, 2 eggs, ½ pint milk and enough flour to make a stiff batter (approximately 2 oz.).
Heat fat in a frying pan; use enough to cover bottom of the pan. Spoon in enough vegetable batter to give a thin layer. Fry until golden on the bottom side—turn and brown on the second side. Serve hot with cold meat or poultry or cheese.

Using the blender:

The blender produces a purée if vegetables are left in the goblet WITH water, but they can be cut into more definite pieces if the following method is used.
Put a cabbage leaf at the bottom of the blender (liquidiser) so it minimises the effectiveness of the blades. Put the vegetables and water into the goblet, switch quickly to high speed for a short time only until vegetables are chopped into tiny pieces. Strain and use in cooking.

Stuffing for vegetables

This quantity is sufficient to stuff:

1 medium sized marrow	4 medium aubergines or
2 large or 4 small peppers	4 large onions

cooking time	see method
blender or mincer speed	medium

For the stuffing:

3 oz. bread	2 medium onions—
parsley—to give two	see stage 2
tablespoons when	3 oz. Cheddar cheese
chopped	1 oz. melted butter
4 large tomatoes	seasoning

1 Put the bread and parsley into the dry goblet and switch gradually to high until a fine mixture.
2 Put the tomatoes, onions—raw—unless stuffing cooked onion, cheese and butter into goblet, switch on until a purée.
3 If using a mincer put bread and onions through this—chop parsley and tomatoes and grate cheese.
4 Mix all ingredients together, season well.

If stuffing aubergines:

Halve aubergines, sprinkle in salt. Stand for 20 minutes. Scoop out centre pulp, either chop finely or put into blender with other ingredients. Pack into aubergine shells. Put in buttered dish, cover with buttered paper and bake for 45 minutes in very moderate oven (300–350°F.—Gas Mark 3–4).

If stuffing marrow:

Peel, halve the marrow, remove seeds, put stuffing into 1 half, cover with the other half. Wrap in very well buttered foil and bake for $1\frac{1}{2}$ hours in middle of moderate oven (350–375°F.—Gas Mark 4–5).

If stuffing onions:

Omit raw onions from stuffing. Peel and boil large onions for nearly 1 hour until becoming soft. Drain, remove centre, put this into blender with tomatoes, etc. Pack mixture into onion cases, put into buttered dish, bake as peppers.

If stuffing peppers:

Halve, remove core and seeds. Simmer the pepper shells in salted water for 5 minutes, strain. Put in stuffing. Bake for 35 minutes in well greased dish in moderate oven (350–375°F.—Gas Mark 4). Cover dish for soft top, leave uncovered for crisp topping.

Salads

When preparing the salad the blender, mincer or shredder and slicer could be used to give even sized pieces of vegetable or fruit.

Most vegetables can be put through the slicer—see previous chapter, but tomatoes, because of their soft texture, cannot be sliced in this way. If put into the blender or through the mincer, slicer or shredder, they immediately become a pulp.

Coleslaw:

Put white cabbage through the slicer—in order to freshen this it should be soaked for a while in very cold water, drained thoroughly. Mix the cabbage with

a chopped nuts (use the blender or shredder), sultanas, and blend with mayonnaise.

b carrots (use the mincer, shredder or grater or the blender—with a little water which is drained away) and capers and blend with oil and vinegar dressing.

c finely chopped spring onions or chives and remoulade sauce (see page 48).

d finely shredded or grated red and green pepper and apple and blend with mayonnaise or oil and vinegar dressing.

Coleslaw made with a blender:

Put the cabbage into the goblet with water to cover. Switch to high speed for about 20 seconds only. Strain and allow to dry for a short time then use as above, selecting any combination of flavours.

Cucumber salad

Put 4 oz. cheese and 2 oz. shelled walnuts into slicer. Cover with lemon juice or vinegar and seasoning or make a sour sweet dressing by blending 2 tablespoons oil, 1 tablespoon white vinegar or lemon juice, $\frac{1}{2}$ teaspoon sugar, seasoning; pour over the cucumber and leave to stand for about 30 minutes before using. Garnish with chopped dill or parsley.

Cheese and walnut salad

Put 4 oz. cheese and 2 oz. shelled walnuts into the blender and leave until finely grated. Blend with 3 tablespoons mayonnaise and a sprinkling of paprika.

Either form into small balls and arrange on a bed of crisp lettuce, garnished with sliced tomatoes, cucumber, etc., or use as a filling in:

a halved well drained canned pears or ripe pears, or

b rings of pineapple or

c halved canned or fresh peaches.

Note:

If using fresh pears or peaches, sprinkle well with lemon juice to prevent the flesh becoming darker in colour.

Potato salad balls

This makes a very pleasant change from an ordinary potato salad. Cook 1 lb. potatoes. Mash the potatoes as page 41, but add no butter or milk, instead beat 2 tablespoons mayonnaise into the smooth potato and add 2 tablespoons chopped chives (these may be chopped in the blender) and 2 medium grated carrots (prepare these in the grater or grinder or the blender—covering with water as for cabbage (see page 45).

Form into balls and top with a little mayonnaise and chopped parsley and paprika pepper.

Jellied salad

cooking time	few minutes
blender speed	high

you will need for 4 servings:

1 small onion	1 green pepper
1 scant pint water	small piece cucumber
1 lemon flavoured jelly	few radishes
juice of ½ fresh lemon	few cooked peas
2 young carrots	

1 Simmer the onion for a few minutes in the water to flavour this, then lift out.
2 Dissolve the lemon flavoured jelly in the hot onion flavoured water, pour into the blender, add the lemon juice.
3 Allow the liquid to cool down, so it does not soften the vegetables.
4 Cut the vegetables into fairly large pieces, put into the goblet with the lemon jelly, omit the peas.
5 Switch to high for about 20–30 seconds only until the vegetables are chopped into tiny pieces.
6 Add the peas, and pour into an oiled mould and allow to set.
Serve with cold meats or cheese and green salad.

Vegetable aspic

As above but dissolve sufficient aspic jelly to set 1 pint in just under 1 pint water. Put into goblet, add lemon juice and proceed as above.

Orange jellied salad

Dissolve sufficient aspic jelly to set 1 pint in ½ pint very hot water. Pour into the blender goblet, allow to cool, then add the pulp from 3 large oranges, together with 2–3 strips of thinly pared orange rind. Switch gradually to high until emulsified. Measure and you should have 1 pint pulp, if less, then add a little water or lemon juice if a sharper jelly is required, or add sugar if a sweeter jelly is required. If by chance the oranges seem very large and juicy then use 2 only. Pour into oiled mould and allow to set. This is delicious served with cold duck, goose or pork.

Cheese and tomato salad loaf

Dissolve ½ oz. powder gelatine in ¼ pint water to which is added 1 tablespoon lemon juice; or use enough aspic jelly to set 1 pint, but dissolve in ¼ pint water only.
Put into the blender goblet with 4 tablespoons mayonnaise, 12 oz. skinned tomatoes and switch on until a smooth pulp. Add 8 oz. Cheddar or Gruyère cheese gradually, 3 medium gherkins and seasoning to taste. Leave until a smooth purée. Put into oiled mould and allow to set. Slice and serve with potato salad and a green salad and mayonnaise.

Cold sauces

Mayonnaise and similar mixtures are very easily made with the help of a mixer. If wished, use the whisk and a bowl, but if you have a choice of mixer or blender, you will probably prefer the latter as it is quicker to use.

Mayonnaise with a whisk

mixer speed   low then high

ingredients as mayonnaise below:

1 Read NOTE right before commencing to make mayonnaise.
2 Put the eggs, seasoning and sugar into a dry bowl, whisk on low speed, adding about 1 tablespoon of the vinegar or lemon juice, until the eggs become slightly 'cloudy'.
3 Gradually add the oil (with some mixers you may have an oil 'dripper' to regulate the flow) and continue as mayonnaise below.
4 Blend in the rest of the vinegar or lemon juice at the end, together with very hot water if wished.

Mayonnaise

blender speed   high then low

you will need for 6–8 servings:

2 egg yolks	pinch sugar
$\frac{1}{4}$ level teaspoon pepper	2–4 tablespoons vinegar
1 level teaspoon salt	or lemon juice
$\frac{1}{4}$ level teaspoon paprika	up to $\frac{1}{2}$ pint oil
1 level teaspoon dry mustard	

1 Make sure the blender goblet is dry, clean and cool before you begin.
2 Put the egg yolks into the goblet, add all the seasonings plus the sugar.
3 Put in half the vinegar or lemon juice and switch on to a high speed for approximately 15 seconds.
4 If using a blender with a cap in the lid, remove this. If not, tilt the lid so the oil may be added without fear of splashing.
5 Add the oil very steadily on a fairly low speed. Continue adding the oil until the mayonnaise is as thick as you like. The more oil that is added, providing it is not put in too quickly, the thicker the mayonnaise will be.
6 Add the rest of the vinegar or lemon juice at the end.

Note:
A tablespoon of very hot water put in at the end gives you a very creamy mayonnaise.

Note:
Half quantities can be made if wished. Realise that this is just as much an art to make in a blender as by hand and, therefore, you must watch the process very carefully. If by chance the mayonnaise shows signs of not thickening or of curdling, stop the blender at once. The only way to remedy this is to pour the mixture out of the goblet, put another egg yolk in, switch on and gradually add the curdled egg and oil mixture until smooth. You may then continue adding the rest of the oil.
Olive oil undoubtedly is the easiest to handle.
If the mayonnaise becomes thick before all the oil is added, stop the blender, taste and add a little vinegar or lemon juice being very careful not to add too much and spoil the flavour.

Green mayonnaise

Make the mayonnaise as recipe above. Add a small sprig of parsley, 1 or 2 leaves of chives, 1 or 2 leaves of sage and a tiny sprig of mint, and any other herbs desired. Put into the blender goblet with the mayonnaise, switch on until the herbs are very finely chopped.

Tomato mayonnaise

Make the mayonnaise as recipe above. Then add two medium sized skinned, halved tomatoes, preferably with the seeds removed. Switch on until a smooth mixture. If using this for fish cocktails, a few drops of Worcestershire sauce, Tabasco sauce, and/or Chilli sauce, a squeeze of lemon juice and a tablespoon of thick cream may all be added at the same time.

Tartare sauce

Ingredients as mayonnaise

small sprig of parsley	1–2 teaspoons capers
2–3 small gherkins	

Make the mayonnaise as recipe above. When blended add all the other ingredients and switch on until finely chopped.
This is served with hot or cold fish, etc.

Remoulade sauce

blender speed   high then low

you will need for 6–8 servings:

2 hard-boiled eggs
1 egg yolk
seasoning
$\frac{1}{2}$–1 tablespoon mustard
(French or English)

1 tablespoon vinegar,
preferably wine vinegar
up to $\frac{1}{2}$ pint olive oil

1 Put the hard-boiled eggs and egg yolk into the blender with seasoning and mustard.
2 Add vinegar and switch on until blended, then gradually add oil as for mayonnaise. This can be used instead of mayonnaise, recipe page 47, adding less mustard if wished.

Cream cheese mayonnaise

Make the mayonnaise as page 47 and add 2 oz. cream cheese when blended, together with 2 tablespoons thin cream and a little extra seasoning. Switch on until a very thick mixture. Excellent with potato salad.

Savoury butters

A savoury butter is used as a garnish on fish, meat or small savouries.
The whisk of a mixer can be used for softening the butter or for blending the ingredients (unless using herbs when it is unsuitable as the parsley, etc., becomes tangled in the blades).
Quantities are sufficient for 4 portions or to garnish about 18 tiny cocktail savouries.

Anchovy butter

Cream 2–3 oz. butter, gradually blend in a few drops anchovy essence. Serve on fish.

Chive butter

Cream 2–3 oz. butter, add 1 tablespoon chopped chives (these may be chopped in the blender). Excellent for jacket potatoes, meat.

Garlic butter

As anchovy butter, but work in 1 crushed clove garlic—to crush this skin the clove (tiny segment), put the clove on a board with a good pinch of salt and crush with the tip of a knife. As salt is used select unsalted butter.
Used as a coating for escargots (snails) or a topping for meat.

Lemon butter

Cream the finely grated rind (yellow 'zest' only) of $\frac{1}{2}$–1 lemon with 2 oz. butter, then blend in $\frac{1}{2}$ tablespoon lemon juice. Serve on fish or veal.

Lobster butter

Buy a hen lobster—this has a wider tail than a cock. Remove the red coral (roe), and blend gradually into 2–3 oz. butter. Serve on fish or canapés.

Maître d'hôtel butter

This is the same as parsley butter and is made by adding 1 tablespoon chopped parsley and 1 teaspoon lemon juice to 2–3 oz. butter. Chill well, cut into neat pats and put on steak, chops, fillets of veal or fish just before serving.

Parsley butter

This is the same as maître d'hôtel butter, above.

Mustard butter

Add a generous pinch cayenne pepper and 2 teaspoons French mustard or blended dry mustard to 2–3 oz. butter. Cream very well. Serve on fish, particularly herrings, or on meat.

Watercress butter

Blend 1–2 teaspoons lemon juice with 2 oz. butter, add 1–2 tablespoons chopped watercress—use a spoon for this.

Worcestershire butter

Blend 1–2 teaspoons Worcestershire sauce into 2–3 oz. butter. Cream very well, add a little chopped watercress or parsley with a spoon.

To clean the whisk after making butters:
Naturally the mixture in the savoury butter above is fairly stiff, so to prevent any being wasted add 2–3 drops of boiling water before trying to remove the mixture from the bowl—this should soften it enough to make it drop from the whisk.
Move the whisk (free from butter) in very hot detergent lather to clean.

Cold desserts

The blender and whisk can be invaluable in preparing desserts. Use the whisk for egg whites, whipping creams and jellies, etc.
Use the blender for making interesting purées of fruit, fruit foule, etc.
You will find that the most delicious desserts are produced in a very short time.

Desserts with fruit

Remember that the fruit mixture will be slightly stiffer than when rubbed through a sieve as you will use all the fruit including skins.
If you require a purée completely free from tiny particles of skin or seeds then you must sieve after putting into the blender—this is quite quickly done. Soft and ripe fruits may be made into a purée when raw, if using a very firm fruit add about a tablespoon water, then put in the fruit.
Do not over-cook fruit for the blender is more efficient than an ordinary sieve and you can make a very smooth purée with even partially cooked fruit, and retain much more of the flavour.
Warning: With a stiff fruit mixture it is important to use a very little liquid and to add this to the goblet before the fruit so that the blades can revolve readily.
Do not over-fill the goblet with the ingredients. Make sure the lid is very firmly in position, and hold this as you switch on. NEVER use the stones of fruit as they could damage the blades.

Fruit foules

If you possess a blender, always blend the ingredients for a fruit foule, because you can emulsify acid fruit and custard or cream without fear of curdling and you avoid the problems of sieving. The Gooseberry Foule is an example of how to make this dish when fruit has to be cooked and the Raspberry Foule of a fruit foule when using ripe dessert fruit.
This dessert is often called a fruit fool.

Gooseberry foule (fool)

cooking time	15 minutes
blender speed	high

you will need for 4 servings:

1 lb. gooseberries	sugar to taste
2–3 tablespoons water*	

for the custard:

1¼ tablespoons custard powder (or a packet to use with 1 pint of milk)	sugar to taste
	few drops green colouring if wished
½ pint milk	

to decorate:
little cream

1 Top and tail the gooseberries and cook with no water if ripe, but a small amount* of water if under-ripe, and the sugar.
2 When soft, put into the warm blender goblet.
3 Meanwhile, blend the custard powder with a little cold milk, bring the rest of the milk to the boil, pour over the blended custard powder, return to the pan and cook until very thick, adding sugar to taste.
4 Put the very thick custard into the blender goblet with the fruit purée, switch gradually to high, until a smooth purée, pour into a dish or dishes and leave to set.
5 Decorate when quite cold with cream.
A little vegetable colouring could be added to give a deeper green colour if wished.
Take great care that the blender speed is brought gradually to high, since the mixture could splash a little.

Raspberry foule

blender speed	high

you will need for 4 servings:

1 lb. ripe raspberries	½ pint thick cream
sugar to taste	

1 Put the raspberries into the blender with the sugar, switch on until smooth.
2 Whip the cream lightly and either put into the blender with the fruit or tip the fruit purée into the whipped cream and blend.
For a more economical dessert, thick custard could be used instead.

More fruit foules

Apple: Peel, slice and cook 1 lb. apples with a little lemon rind and juice to taste. Continue as gooseberry foule; sweeten well.

Blackcurrant: Since these have such a concentrated flavour, rather less than 1 lb. fruit could be used. Cook approximately 12 oz. blackcurrants with little if any water and sugar to taste. Proceed as gooseberry foule.

Damson: Since these have such a concentrated flavour, rather less than 1 lb. fruit could be used. Stones *must* be removed before putting the fruit into the blender goblet.

Rhubarb: Cook 1 lb. rhubarb with no water and with sugar to taste, continue as gooseberry foule.

Fruit snow 1

blender speed	high
mixer speed	high

Use this method for soft fruit like: raspberries, strawberries, etc.

you will need for 4 servings:

approximately 1 lb. fruit	2 egg whites
sugar to taste	

1 Put the fruit with sugar to taste into the blender goblet and make a purée.
2 Measure the pulp and allow 2 egg whites to each $\frac{3}{4}$ pint pulp if wishing to have a very light 'fluffy' mixture or 2 egg whites to 1 pint pulp for a firmer one.
3 Whisk the egg whites until very stiff; if the 'snow' is to stand it is better if 1 oz. castor sugar is whisked into the egg whites when they are very firm.
4 Gradually fold the egg whites into the fruit purée. Put into glasses.

Fruit snow 2

Use this method for firm fruits

cooking time	as fruit see Stage 1
blender speed	high
mixer speed	high

quantities as above

1 Cook the fruit with sugar to taste and the minimum of water. If it is possible to cook this in a double saucepan it is a good idea, then there is no possibility of the fruit burning.
2 Method as above; if by chance the fruit has made more juice than expected strain this away and use as a sauce or in making a jelly.

Raspberry Bavarian

cooking time	few minutes
blender speed	medium or high

you will need for 4 servings:

1 raspberry flavoured jelly	$\frac{1}{4}$ pint cream (thin cream
$\frac{1}{2}$ pint water	could be used)
6 oz. fresh, canned* or	little extra sugar if wished
frozen raspberries	

to decorate:
thick cream, fruit

*Use syrup in place of some water.

1 Either dissolve the jelly in the hot water or pour the very hot water into the blender goblet, adding the jelly, broken into pieces.
2 Switch on until blended, then cool slightly and add fruit and cream, with extra sugar if wished.
3 Switch on and leave until smooth, allow any bubbles to subside.
4 Pour into glasses, a shallow dish or a mould and allow to set.
5 Decorate with cream and fruit.

Fresh fruit jelly

cooking time	few minutes
blender speed	medium or high

you will need for 4 servings:

about 8–10 oz. fresh	sugar to taste
raspberries, strawberries,	$\frac{1}{2}$ oz. powder gelatine or
or other ripe fruit (or	amount needed to set
approximately $\frac{1}{2}$ pint	1 pint
purée)	$\frac{1}{2}$ pint water

1 Put fruit into goblet—you need $\frac{1}{2}$ pint purée, together with sugar to taste.
2 Blend the gelatine with 2 tablespoons cold water.
3 Stir into the very hot water and tip into the warmed blender goblet.

4 Switch on until blended with fruit.

5 Allow to stand for a while for the bubbles on top to subside, then pour into a dish or mould to set.

Fruit jelly whip

mixer speed   low, then high

you will need for 4 servings:

1 fruit flavoured jelly   ¼ pint thick cream
¾ pint water   little fresh fruit

1 Make the jelly in the usual way but with ¾ pint liquid only, this can be all water or use water and some fruit juice.

2 Allow to set, but do not leave until too firm.

3 Whip the cream in the bowl on low speed until it just thickens slightly, do not over-whip otherwise it will become like butter.

4 Gradually whip in the jelly until very light and fluffy, the speed can be increased when there is no possibility of the mixture splashing.

5 Fold in fresh fruit if wished.

7 ways to make easy fruit desserts

Apple 'tipsy'

quantity for 4 people

Put approximately ¾ pint thick apple purée into the blender, add 2 oz. walnuts, 2 oz. coconut, 2 oz. stale cake (broken into pieces) and 2 tablespoons brandy. Switch on until blended. Put in glasses and top with cream and nuts—try this with apricots or other fruit.

Banana 'flummery'

Put 4 ripe, but unblemished bananas into the blender with 2 tablespoons sugar, 1 tablespoon lemon juice, 1 tablespoon white wine. Switch on until a smooth pulp then blend with ½ pint lightly whipped cream. Put into glasses, top with chopped nuts.

Meringue fingers

Fry 8 slices of stale sponge cake in 2 oz. hot butter until crisp and golden. Roll in sugar. Top with ½ pint thick fruit purée, then whisk 2 egg whites until stiff, fold in 2 oz. sugar, pile on the fingers and brown under a hot grill.

Pineapple whip

Strain the juice from a medium can pineapple, measure and add enough water to give ¾ pint. Dissolve a pineapple or lemon jelly in this, put into blender with the fruit from the can. Switch on until smoothly blended. Allow to become half set, then fold in about 2 oz. halved glacé cherries and halved walnuts, put into a mould to set.

Cherry whip

First whip ¼ pint cream with the mixer until it holds its shape. Whisk 2 egg whites until very stiff, fold into the cream with 1 oz. icing sugar. Blend with ½ lb. stoned fresh ripe cherries or well drained canned cherries. Other fruit can be used instead, but this is particularly good with the very black cherries. Serve with sponge fingers.

Stuffed peaches

Put 2 oz. blanched almonds or walnuts, 2 oz. stale sweet biscuits (macaroons ideal) into the blender goblet, switch on until finely chopped. Meanwhile whisk ¼ pint thick cream, fold in the crumbs and nuts, with 1 oz. sieved icing sugar and 1 tablespoon cherry brandy. Put into well drained canned peaches or halved fresh peaches.

Stuffed pears

Use recipe above, but substitute ginger nut crumbs and hazel nuts and flavour with apricot brandy, if wished. Use to stuff pear halves.

Whisking egg whites

One of the most successful jobs that can be done with an electric whisk is to beat egg whites until stiff for meringues, soufflés, etc. It is important, however, to realise the essential facts about successful whipping of egg whites.

a Egg whites will not whip successfully if less than 24 hours old.

b The bowl in which they are to be whisked MUST be absolutely free from the tiniest particles of grease, egg yolk, etc.

c Check also that the whisk of the mixer is dry, clean and no grease is on this.

d If eggs are normally stored in the refrigerator, allow to stand at room temperature for 1 hour before whisking.

e Where you have a choice of speed, a high speed can be used for whisking the egg whites until stiff.

f Switch on and leave until the egg whites stand in peaks—the ways to test if they are sufficiently stiff are:

1. If the bowl could be turned upside down, without the egg white falling out.

2. If a small coin wrapped in greaseproof paper (for hygienic reasons) can be balanced on top of the peaks.

With practice one can tell if sufficiently whisked by looking carefully. Remember however that egg whites CAN be over-whisked, and if this happens the meringues tend to crumble or the cakes (Angel cake) will be too dry, unless a good amount of water is added.

g **It is just as important to add sugar carefully to egg whites when making meringues as it is when doing this by hand.**

1 The sugar is added gradually with the mixer on a low speed, i.e. it is all whipped in.

2 A second way is to add half the sugar in this manner then fold in the remainder by hand— this gives a softer meringue ideal for topping a dessert.

3 All the sugar may be folded in by hand—this gives the softest type of meringue, excellent for adding to chiffon mixtures.

Never over-beat the mixture when once all the sugar has been incorporated.

Quick chocolate mousse

cooking time	few minutes
mixer speed	low for chocolate mixture, high for egg whites

you will need for 4 servings:

4 oz. chocolate (most people prefer plain)	2 eggs
2 dessertspoons sugar	2 dessertspoons thick cream

1 Grate the chocolate.

2 Put the sugar, chocolate and egg yolks in a basin over hot water and whisk together until smooth. (If you have no portable whisk, then beat with a wooden spoon.)

3 Cool slightly, then add cream.

4 When quite cold fold in the stiffly beaten egg whites.

5 Pour into glasses and serve with biscuits.

Coffee chocolate mousse

Use 1 tablespoon coffee essence instead of cream and add a little extra sugar if wished.

Chocolate brandy mousse

Use 1 tablespoon brandy in place of the cream.

Orange chocolate mousse

Put the grated rind of 1 large orange in with the chocolate and blend with 1 tablespoon orange juice instead of cream.

Fruit mousse

cooking time	depending upon fruit
blender speed	high
mixer speed	high

you will need for 4 servings:

approximately 12 oz. fruit	2 tablespoons water
2 oz. sugar	2 eggs
very little water	
2 level teaspoons powder gelatine	

1 Cook the fruit with sugar and a very little water, with very juicy fruit there is no need to add water.
2 Soften the gelatine in the cold water, stir into the hot fruit mixture.
3 Put the fruit and gelatine into the blender goblet and switch on until smooth, then add the egg yolks and blend thoroughly.
4 Allow this mixture to cool, and begin to stiffen very slightly, then fold in the whisked egg whites. Pile into glasses.

Cold sweet soufflé

cooking time	few minutes
mixer speed	high

you will need for 6 servings:

3 eggs	$1\frac{1}{2}$ level dessertspoons powder gelatine
3 oz. sugar	
1 teaspoon vanilla essence	3 tablespoons water
$\frac{1}{2}$ pint milk	12 tablespoons thick cream

to decorate:

4 tablespoons thick cream (buy $\frac{1}{2}$ pint for dessert and decoration)	nuts, angelica, glacé cherries, crystallised rose or violet petals

1 Put the egg yolks, sugar, vanilla and milk into the top of a double saucepan or basin over hot water. If you have a portable whisk then use this instead of a wooden spoon and whisk or stir well until mixture coats back of a wooden spoon.
2 Soften gelatine in the water, then dissolve over hot water.
3 Stir into custard, then when cool, fold in whipped cream—it should hold its shape but if too stiff the soufflé tends to be a little solid.
4 Allow to thicken slightly, meanwhile whisk egg whites until very stiff.
5 Fold into custard and gelatine mixture.

6 Pour into a soufflé dish, with a band of buttered paper tied firmly round outside, standing several inches above level of dish so that soufflé mixture itself more than fills dish and does not overflow.
7 When quite firm decorate with a narrow border of whipped cream and tiny pieces of nut, angelica, glacé cherry, crystallised rose or violet petals. Lastly, carefully remove band of paper.

Almond
Use almond essence instead of vanilla and fold 2 oz. very finely chopped blanched or blanched and browned almonds into the mixture when it begins to stiffen, BEFORE adding the egg whites.

Brandy
Dissolve the gelatine in brandy instead of water. All other liqueurs can be used in the same way—the most delicious are crème de menthe, apricot brandy, etc.

Lemon
Add finely grated rind of 1 lemon to the egg yolks. Dissolve gelatine in hot lemon juice instead of water.

Chocolate
Add 1–2 oz. chocolate to the egg yolks.

Coffee
Dissolve the gelatine in slightly diluted coffee essence or very strong coffee.

Fruit soufflé

cooking time	depending upon fruit
blender speed	high
mixer speed	high

Ingredients as cold sweet soufflé, but omit the milk, instead use approximately $\frac{1}{2}$ pint thick fruit purée, apricots, damsons, blackcurrants are all excellent.

1 Cook the fruit with the sugar (included in the recipe) and the minimum of water, put into the blender goblet until a purée. Sieve in the case of fruits with pips such as blackcurrants. Ripe raspberries or similar fruit should just be blended with the sugar and heated for a few minutes only. Whisk the HOT fruit purée on to the egg yolks (which should be whisked until light and fluffy).
2 Continue as cold sweet soufflé.

Meringue flan – often called a PAVLOVA

cooking time   about 3–4 hours
mixer speed   high then low

you will need for 8 servings:

4 egg whites   8 oz. sugar (see under
                           Meringues, page 75)

1 Line tin with a round or shape of greased greaseproof paper (use butter or oil).
2 Put egg whites into mixer bowl and proceed as for meringues.
3 Pipe or shape into the desired round or square on to the paper on the tin.
4 Bake for 3–4 hours in very cool oven (225–250°F.—Gas Mark ¼–1).
5 Cool slightly, then remove from baking tin.
6 Store in a tin until needed, then fill with ice cream, fruit or whisked fruit or jelly and cream.

Cream sweets

Bavaroise or Bavarian cream

cooking time   15–20 minutes
mixer speed   low

you will need:

4 egg yolks   2–3 tablespoons cold water
4 oz. icing sugar   ¼–½ teaspoon vanilla
½ pint milk   essence
1 level dessertspoon ½ pint whipped cream
  powder gelatine—do
  not exceed this

1 Beat the egg yolks with the sugar, add the hot but not boiling milk and cook in the top of a double saucepan until a smooth thick custard.
2 Soften the gelatine in the water, then dissolve over hot water.
3 Add to the custard together with the vanilla essence and stir over heat until thickened.
4 If using a portable mixer, whisk the egg yolks as they cook with the milk, etc. If using a bigger mixer, stir with a wooden spoon but when the custard has thickened, it lightens this and prevents a skin forming if it is tipped into the mixer bowl and whisked for approximately ½ minute.
If preferred, however, the custard can be put into the blender to make sure it is very smooth. This does, however, tend to make it a little thinner so the custard should be cooked until rather thicker than usual before going into the blender.
5 Allow to cool but not set then fold in the whipped cream.
6 Serve in glasses or put into a mould and turn out when set.

3 easy cream sweets to give 4–5 servings each

Lemon whip

Boil a large can of evaporated milk in boiling water for 15 minutes, open carefully, put in bowl. Dissolve 1 teaspoon powder gelatine in 2 tablespoons lemon juice in a basin over hot water. Add to the evaporated milk. Chill thoroughly then whisk at low speed until mixture starts to thicken, add sugar to taste and whisk at higher speed until light and fluffy.

Syllabub

Whisk ½ pint cream until it begins to hold its shape, then gradually whisk in 1–2 oz. icing sugar, ½ tablespoon lemon juice, 1–2 tablespoons white wine. Whisk 2 egg whites until very stiff. Fold into cream mixture. Serve in shallow glasses.

Zabaione

A small portable whisk is ideal for this delicious Italian sweet. Whisk 3 egg yolks and 1–2 oz. sugar until thickened over a pan of hot water. Gradually whisk in 2–3 tablespoons Marsala. Serve warm or cool. This quantity gives 4–5 servings if put over fruit; but only 2–3 servings by itself.

The blender for whipping cream
Normally one uses a whisk to whip cream, but there are some modern blenders (liquidisers) where the speed on low *is* sufficiently SLOW to whip cream.
Watch carefully as you do this so it does NOT become over-whipped.

Iced desserts

As refrigerators and home freezers become more plentiful, iced and frosted sweets become more and more plentiful.

The use of the mixer in making ice cream

Quick freezing is one secret of success in making cream ices – but efficient whisking is another secret, so that the mixture becomes light and fluffy; too solid an ice cream is NOT enjoyable.

The blender makes sieving or emulsifying fruit both speedy and simple.

Basic ice cream

mixer speed   low then high

you need for 4–5 servings:*

¼ pint thick cream and ¼ pint thin cream or ½ pint whipped evaporated milk	2 oz. sieved icing sugar flavouring 2 egg whites

*Dependent on amount of flavouring used.

Using the whisk

1 Whip the thick cream until it begins to hold a shape, then add the thin cream and whip together—never allow this to become so thick that it is stiff, or the ice cream will be too solid.

2 Fold in the sugar and flavouring, unless advised to the contrary, as some flavourings are put in at Stage 3.
If using evaporated milk follow the directions on the can for whipping, in some cases boil as the recipe for Lemon whip opposite (but omit the lemon juice), in other cases the evaporated milk just needs chilling well THEN whipping. Use a low speed until it starts to stiffen then the speed of the mixer can be increased.

3 Freeze the mixture lightly; meanwhile whisk the egg whites until very stiff, whisk the ice cream mixture until sufficiently soft and light to absorb the egg whites. Then fold these in carefully and slowly.

4 Return to the freezing trays and compartment and continue to freeze until firm.

Note:
The cold control on the refrigerator can be turned to the coldest setting ½ an hour before freezing, it is a good idea to do this with all refrigerators, but particularly important with older models where the freezing compartment is less cold than in the modern models.

Using the blender

As stated opposite some blenders can be used to whip cream, but in most goblets it is possible to emulsify cream plus fruit to give a smooth as well as very light texture.

Follow the recipes for fruit ice creams and put the cream into the goblet, switch to lowest speed until thickened SLIGHTLY ONLY. Add the fruit, increase the speed to medium until emulsified then continue as the recipe. Sugar should be added with the fruit.

Banana ice cream

blender speed   high
whisk speed   see method

you will need for 4 servings:

2 large ripe (but not discoloured) bananas 1 dessertspoon lemon juice 2 oz. icing sugar ½ teaspoon vanilla essence	3 tablespoons milk or thin cream ¼ pint thick cream or whipped evaporated milk 2 egg whites few drops cochineal (optional)

1 Put bananas, lemon juice and sugar into blender goblet, switch to high until smooth purée, add vanilla essence.

2 Pour into a bowl. If any purée is left in goblet add the milk or thin cream and switch on to make it easier to remove.

3 Add the lightly whipped cream.

4 Put into freezing tray and freeze on coldest position for approximately 35 minutes.

5 Put into bowl and whisk lightly, then fold in the stiffly beaten egg whites (use high speed to whisk these).

6 Return to freezing tray and freeze until firm, then return indicator to normal setting to store.
If wished this ice cream can be coloured with a very few drops of cochineal.

Fruit ice cream

Either use the raspberry ice cream, below, as a basic recipe or Basic Ice Cream, on page 55, and add a good ¼ pint fruit purée.

Pineapple crumb ice cream

First make crumbs of 2 medium macaroon biscuits. Then put the well drained fruit from small can of pineapple cubes or rings, after removing biscuits from goblet, into the blender. Add about 3 tablespoons syrup, switch on until pineapple begins to form a purée. Switch off then add 3 oz. maraschino cherries plus 1–2 tablespoons of syrup. Switch on again until these are chopped. Add to the whipped cream and sugar.

Raspberry ice cream

| blender speed | high |
| whisk speed | see method |

you will need for 4 servings:

8 oz. fresh fruit or 1 packet	¼ pint thick cream
frozen raspberries or	2 egg whites
1 medium-sized can	few drops cochineal,
2 tablespoons sugar	if wished

1 Put the fruit into the blender goblet, switch to high until smooth.
2 Pour into a bowl. If any purée is left in the goblet add 1 tablespoon milk and switch on to make it easier to remove.
3 Add the sugar and the lightly whipped cream—use low speed for this.
4 Pour into freezing tray and freeze on coldest setting for approximately 30 minutes.
5 Put into bowl, whip lightly, then fold in the stiffly beaten whites of the eggs (use high speed to whisk these) and cochineal, if desired.
6 Return to the freezing trays and freeze until firm, then turn cold control to normal setting to store.

Strawberry ice cream

Use strawberries in place of raspberries.

Fruit ripple ice creams

These fruit ripple ice creams are delicious.

First prepare the ripple mixture as this must be fairly stiff.
Put 8 oz. fruit—raspberries, strawberries or other fairly strongly flavoured fruit into the blender. Make a smooth purée, add 2 oz. sugar and 1 teaspoon powder gelatine dissolved in 2 tablespoons water, orange or lemon juice or fruit syrup, if using canned, defrosted frozen fruit, or cooked fruit. To dissolve the gelatine put this into a basin over very hot water. Switch on the blender until fruit and gelatine are well blended. Tip out and allow to become cold, then freeze very lightly.
Meanwhile, prepare the basic ice cream and freeze to Stage 4, until it just holds a shape but is not too stiff.
Take this out of the refrigerator, do not remove from the freezing trays.
Spoon the fruit mixture through this, beating lightly to get a good distribution of the fruit—do not try to mix—you should have distinct layers of fruit and ice cream.

Suggested combination of flavours for fruit ripple ice creams

Use basic ice cream recipe.

Apricot and almond

Fruit: Use apricots flavoured with little lemon.
Ice cream: Flavour with almond essence and add 2–3 chopped blanched almonds.

Apricot and chocolate

Fruit: Use apricots flavoured with a tablespoon apricot brandy.
Ice cream: Add 3 oz. cool melted chocolate to ice cream at Stage 2 or use 2 oz. chocolate powder and ½ teaspoon vanilla essence.

Apple and coffee

Fruit: Use cooked apples, flavoured with little chopped preserved ginger.
Ice cream: Use vanilla or coffee flavoured.
To make the latter add 1 tablespoon coffee essence at Stage 2.

Blackcurrant and strawberry

Fruit: Use blackcurrants (these can be sieved if wished).
Ice cream: Blend $\frac{1}{4}$ pint strawberry purée with basic ice cream at Stage 2.

Caramel ripple

Caramel: Boil a small can condensed milk in water for 2 hours, allow to cool, and use as the filling.
Ice cream: Excellent with vanilla, chocolate or coffee.

Orange

Fruit: Put the pulp from 3–4 large oranges into the blender, flavour with curaçao if wished, add sugar and gelatine.
Ice cream: Vanilla or chocolate.

Raspberry

Fruit layer: Use raspberries, sweeten well so the fruit layer does not become too stiff.
Ice cream: Use vanilla or strawberry.

Strawberry

Fruit layer: As raspberry, using strawberries on their own, or a mixture of raspberries and strawberries.

Less usual ice creams

All of these are the quantity for the basic ice cream page 55.

Brown bread ice cream

This sounds a very strange flavouring, but it is delicious.
Put 2–3 oz. brown bread (free from crusts) into the goblet and make fine crumbs. Either use these as soft crumbs or put into the oven for a short time until they are golden brown then blend with the basic ice cream mixture at Stage 2.

Carrot ice cream

Again a very unusual blending of flavours. Choose young sweet carrots, peel or scrape very carefully. Put 3 oz. into the blender with milk to cover. Switch on until smoothly emulsified. Use all thick cream in the basic ice cream, since this will be diluted with the carrot-milk mixture. Add this at Stage 2.
Taste carefully and add a little cinnamon if wished to give a 'bite' to the mixture or flavour with finely grated lemon rind.
2–3 oz. chopped nuts are excellent added to this particular ice cream.

Marshmallow and raisin

Put $\frac{1}{4}$ pint hot milk into the hot blender with 4 oz. marshmallows (pink if possible). Switch on for a short time only—the marshmallows should be partially chopped and emulsified.
Allow to cool then add to the basic ice cream at Stage 2—it is advisable to fold the whipped cream into the marshmallow mixture, not the other way round. Add 2–3 oz. seedless raisins.
This can be varied a great deal, use chopped nuts; 4 oz. chopped pineapple; 2–3 crumbled macaroon biscuits; 3–4 oz. maraschino cherries; or use a mixture of all the ingredients to give a Tutti-fruitti ice cream.

Prune ice cream

Soak and cook about 6 oz. prunes, **remove stones.** Put into the blender with about $\frac{1}{4}$ pint of the cooking liquid and a few strips thinly pared lemon rind. Switch on until a smooth purée. Blend with the cream at Stage 2. 2 oz. blanched chopped almonds could be added.

Water ices and sorbets

These delicious mixtures are refreshing and easily made.

Water ices

mixer speed	high
blender speed	low then high

4–5 servings

use 1 lb. fruit	lemon juice if wished
½ pint water	1 teaspoon powdered
sugar to taste	gelatine
	1 egg white

1 Simmer the fruit with the water and sugar to give a fairly sweet taste, if the fruit has not a particularly sharp flavour then add a little lemon juice.
2 Dissolve the gelatine in the hot fruit.
3 Tip into the warmed blender goblet, switch on until a smooth purée, cool.
4 Freeze until just setting, then whisk and fold in the stiffly beaten egg white.

For fruit juice water ices

Either use the juice from 2–3 oranges or 2–3 lemons and simmer the peel with ½ pint water then proceed as above, or remember with a blender you can use all the purée of the fresh oranges to give a thicker fruit ice.

Simmer the peel from the oranges with ½ pint water for 10 minutes, dissolve the gelatine in this. Put the pulp from 3 large oranges into the blender goblet, add the strained liquid, sugar to taste and switch on until smooth. Continue as water ice above.

Sorbets

Make these in the same way as water ices, but use 2–3 egg whites to the amount of fruit purée, so giving a lighter mixture.

Note:

The gelatine is not essential but this is an advantage if keeping the sorbet, etc., for any length of time as it helps to prevent the mixture forming little 'splinters' of ice.

Unusual flavours for water ices and sorbets, try:
Blackberry and apple: Use equal quantities of the fruits.

Damson: Sweeten well and take care all stones are removed before putting into goblet. Use the sieve for this if you have such an attachment on your particular mixer, as this saves removing the stones by hand.
Gooseberry: Use either green or ripe gooseberries.
Melon: Simmer the peel with the water and the juice of 1 lemon, sweeten well and increase the gelatine to 1½ teaspoons. Put the pulp into the goblet with the strained liquid and proceed as before. If rather colourless, a few drops of apple green colouring makes this look better.

Frosted fruit mousse

blender speed	high
whisk speed	high

you will need for 4 servings:

1 lb. fruit (weight when peeled or stoned)	grated rind and juice 1 lemon
¼ pint water	½ pint cream or evaporated milk
3 oz. sugar	

1 Cook the fruit with the water and sugar until soft.
2 Put into warmed blender goblet. Switch gradually to high, add lemon juice and rind (this may be put into blender first or put with the fruit).
3 Cool, then fold in the lightly whipped evaporated milk or cream.
4 Spoon into the freezing trays, and freeze on coldest setting until just firm, then return control to normal setting to store.

If wished 1 or 2 stiffly beaten egg whites can be added *after* the cream, in which case you may care to add a little extra sugar.

Note:

With soft berry fruits use 3 tablespoons water only.

Frosted Bavarians

Use the recipe for the Bavarian creams as recipes on pages 50 and 54, and frost this lightly. Do not allow to become as firm as an ice cream otherwise the creamy taste is lost.

Frosted soufflés

The cold cream and fruit soufflés lend themselves to frosting, see page 53.

Make and prepare the soufflés—use soufflé dishes that will stand in the freezing compartment without fear of their breaking in any way.

Frost for a short time only; the time, of course, will depend upon the type of refrigerator, or if you are using a home freezer—allow about 25 minutes in a domestic refrigerator of the modern type, 45 minutes in an older type or about 20 minutes in the home freezer—a little less for the fruit soufflé.

Baked Alaska of all kinds

A baked Alaska is a combination of ice cream and meringue. The secret of success is to coat the *VERY FIRM* ice cream with *VERY STIFF* meringue and brown this in the oven for a short time only, at a VERY HIGH TEMPERATURE.

Baked Alaska

cooking time	3–5 minutes
blender speed	high

you will need for 4–6 servings:

6–7 inch round sponge cake	medium-sized block ice cream
4 egg whites	little fresh, canned or frozen fruit
4–8 oz. sugar—see Stage 2	

1 Put the sponge cake on an ovenproof plate.
2 Put the egg whites in the mixer bowl, whisk until very stiff, add the sugar—see remarks on page 52. The amount of sugar varies according to personal taste.
3 Arrange the ice cream on the sponge with a little fruit at the sides and on top.
4 Cover the sponge, ice cream and fruit completely with the meringue.
5 Put for a few minutes only in a very hot oven (475–500°F.—Gas Mark 9–10); watch carefully to see the meringue does not burn.
6 Serve at once—but it will stand for 20–25 minutes without the ice cream melting.

Almond Alaska

Make a 'bed' of macaroon biscuits. Cover these with well-drained canned apricots and shredded almonds. Top with vanilla ice cream and meringue and press flaked almonds into this. Brown in very hot oven for 3–5 minutes as above.

Banana cream Alaska

Put 4 bananas and 3 tablespoons thick cream into the blender with 1 oz. sugar and a squeeze lemon juice, switch to high until a thick purée. Spread a 7–8 inch sponge flan—recipe page 73, with lemon curd or apricot jam, top with banana cream, ice cream and meringue and brown in very hot oven.

Omelette surprise

This can be another name for Baked Alaska or is made as follows:

Put the ice cream in the dish—it can stand on sponge or this can be omitted. Top with fruit. Whisk 3 egg yolks with 1 oz. sugar until thick. Whisk 4 egg whites until very stiff, adding 4 oz. sugar as for meringue; fold into egg yolks. Spread gently over the ice cream and fruit and brown for 3 minutes in very hot oven.

Cold sweet sauces

A cold sauce is an excellent topping for ice creams, moulds such as blancmange, or to serve with a plain cold soufflé or Bavarian cream.

The following recipes provide quickly-made cold sauces.

Apricot

Put small can apricots, the syrup from can and 2 tablespoons apricot jam into blender, switch to high until emulsified.

Try adding

a) blanched almonds; b) glacé or maraschino cherries; c) lemon juice to flavour, and use lemon curd instead of apricot jam.

Other fruits may be used instead:

1 Cooked apples—flavour with orange or ginger marmalade.
2 Bananas—blend $\frac{1}{4}$ pint orange juice, 4 bananas, and 2 tablespoons sugar or apricot jam.
3 Cherries—stone cherries and blend with syrup from can, little cherry brandy and 2 tablespoons redcurrant jelly.
4 Orange—use pulp of 3–4 oranges, 3 tablespoons water, sugar to taste and/or 1–2 tablespoons orange marmalade.
5 Lemon—use pulp of 2 lemons, 4 tablespoons water, 2 oz. sugar and 2 tablespoons lemon or orange marmalade.
6 Peaches, pineapple, plums, etc.—as apricots.

Melba sauce

cooking time	few minutes
blender speed	high

you will need for 4 servings:

6 oz. fresh, frozen or canned raspberries	1 tablespoon castor sugar
1 level teaspoon cornflour	3 tablespoons redcurrant or apple jelly
2 tablespoons water OR fruit syrup from canned or frozen fruit	

1 Put the raspberries into the blender goblet, switch on until smooth.
2 Blend the cornflour with the water or syrup.
3 Put into a saucepan with the other ingredients, including the fruit.
4 Cook very gently on a very low heat until thick.
5 Return to the blender goblet to give a smooth sauce, allow to cool.

By blending the raspberries first, the sauce cooks in the shortest possible time and you retain the maximum flavour of the fruit.

Mock cream with evaporated milk

mixer speed	medium

Boil the tin of milk in a pan for 15 minutes. Put into a cold place for several hours, overnight in the refrigerator is ideal. Turn into a large bowl and whisk until thick and fluffy.

Mock cream

cooking time	10 minutes
mixer speed	low to medium

you will need:

1 tablespoon cornflour	1–2 oz. butter
$\frac{1}{4}$ pint milk	1 oz. castor sugar

Blend cornflour to a smooth mixture with the milk, put into a saucepan and bring slowly to the boil, stirring all the time. Cook until thick. Allow to become quite cool. Cream the butter and sugar until very soft. **On no account warm the butter.** Gradually beat in spoonfuls of the cornflour mixture. The more you beat this the better the cream becomes.

Mock cream with a blender

Follow the recipe above, but put *cold* cornflour mixture, etc., into blender, switch gradually to high.

This gives a less thick cream but an excellent consistency.

Fruit cream sauces

Use recipes as fruit sauces opposite, but omit some of the syrup from canned, frozen or cooked fruit and use thick or thin cream.

Chocolate sauce

Put 6–8 oz. plain chocolate, broken into pieces, and 4–6 tablespoons milk or thin cream into the blender. Switch gradually to high until blended. If wished, the milk could be hot.

Fatless 'cream'

mixer speed	high

1 egg white	1 tablespoon warmed golden syrup

1 Put the egg white into the mixer bowl, and whisk until very thick.
2 Gradually add the golden syrup.

This cream is ideal for anyone on a 'fat free' diet.

Hard-sauce or Brandy butter

mixer speed   low to medium

you will need for 5–6 servings:

4 oz. butter, preferably   6 oz. sieved icing sugar
    unsalted   2–3 tablespoons brandy

1 Cream the butter and icing sugar until soft and light in texture.
2 Add the brandy gradually – this is important to prevent the mixture curdling.
3 Pile or pipe into a neat pyramid and chill.
This may be decorated with leaves of angelica, halved cherries, or blanched almonds.
Serve with Christmas pudding.

Hot sauces

Remember that custard (made with custard powder) has a wonderfully smooth texture when emulsified in the blender before being served or put on to a trifle. If a skin has formed, this will disappear after being in the blender.
An egg custard sauce can also be emulsified before serving; this is particularly useful if the sauce has curdled slightly.
A custard or similar sauce will always be a little thinner in texture after being put into the blender.

Fruit sauces

cooking time   depending on sauce
blender speed   high

you will need for 4–5 servings:

approximately 1 lb. fruit   water
sugar to taste

1 Simmer fruit with sugar and water to give a reasonable amount of syrup until fruit is soft.
2 Tip into hot blender goblet and switch gradually to high until smooth.
3 If serving at once there is no need to blend with cornflour, but if allowing the sauce to stand, add 2 teaspoons cornflour or arrowroot, blended with 3–4 tablespoons water (or fresh orange or lemon juice) at Stage 1, when the fruit is tender and simmer until the syrup is smooth and clear.

Chocolate sauce

cooking time   10 minutes
blender speed   high

you will need for 4 servings:

1 oz. cornflour   3 oz. plain chocolate
1 pint milk   1 oz. butter
1–2 oz. sugar

1 Blend the cornflour with a little cold milk.
2 Heat the rest of the milk and sugar, pour over the blended cornflour.
3 Put into pan and cook until thickened.
4 Tip into warmed blender with the chocolate and butter.
5 Switch on until smoothly blended. Serve at once, or keep hot in the top of a double saucepan, covering the sauce with buttered paper to prevent a skin forming.
Serve with ice cream—chocolate puddings, etc.

Raisin walnut sauce

cooking time   5 minutes
blender speed   high

you will need for 4 servings:

6 oz. raisins   1–2 tablespoons brandy
juice of 2 oranges   2 oz. walnuts, shelled
¼ pint water

1 Heat all ingredients except nuts for 5 minutes.
2 Tip into warmed blender goblet, switch on until raisins make thick purée.
3 Drop in nuts, switch on again for a short time.
Serve with ice cream—hot puddings.

Hot Puddings

A mixer, a blender and occasionally a mincer are of value when making hot puddings. The recipes below give an idea of some of the puddings that can be made more easily, efficiently and successfully with a mixer, but you will be able to experiment with many of your own favourite recipes.

For example in a rich fruit pudding, the richest of all being a Christmas pudding, the mincer gives an excellent blending of ingredients. While it is certainly not essential to mince the fruit it does produce a particularly delicious pudding.

Many hot puddings are based on a creamed sponge and suggestions for this type of pudding are given together with rather unusual toppings which could not be made without the help of a blender, or would be extremely troublesome to make.

Meringues are part of many puddings and it is advisable to read the comments on page 52 about whisking egg whites with the mixer.

Sponge pudding

cooking time $1\frac{1}{4}$ hours
mixer speed   low to medium

you will need for 4–6 servings:

Ingredients as Victoria sandwich, page 75 using 4 oz. margarine or butter, etc., and method of mixing as given. For instructions on cooking the sponge, toppings, etc., see below. To cook the sponge pudding

1 Grease and flour a $1\frac{1}{2}$–2 pint basin.
2 Put in the topping – see opposite.
3 Put in the sponge mixture – always allow room in the basin for the pudding to rise.
4 Cover with greased greaseproof paper and/or foil.
5 Put in a steamer over boiling water and cook quickly to give a really light pudding, for 1 hour, after this time the heat could be reduced slightly but always fill up with boiling water.
6 Turn out and serve with custard or a hot sauce.

Christmas pudding

Many people like a Christmas pudding where all the ingredients are minced so they blend into a very moist mixture.
Here is a recipe suitable for that.
Before mincing:
a Stone raisins (do this with damp fingers—the stones are easier to remove).
b Put the bread through the mincer BEFORE the moist ingredients, follow that with the suet, nuts, lemon rind, then you can add the more moist foods, ending with the apple, which is very soft.

cooking time   6–8 hours, plus 2 hours re-steaming
mincer speed   medium, then low for the very soft ingredients

you will need for 1 large or 2 smaller puddings:

4 oz. flour	4 oz. sultanas
2 oz. breadcrumbs	2 oz. chopped prunes or
1 teaspoon mixed spice	dried apricots
1 level teaspoon cinnamon	4 oz. chopped blanched
1 level teaspoon nutmeg	almonds
4 oz. shredded suet	grated rind $\frac{1}{2}$ lemon,
4 oz. brown sugar	juice $\frac{1}{2}$ lemon
4 oz. grated apple	grated rind $\frac{1}{2}$ orange
1 small grated carrot	1 tablespoon golden syrup
4 oz. mixed candied peel	or black treacle
2 eggs	$\frac{1}{4}$ pint ale, beer, stout or
4 oz. currants	milk
8 oz. raisins	

1 Mix all ingredients together, stir well and leave overnight if possible.
2 Place in one large or 2 smaller basins and cover well with cloth or paper.
3 Steam or boil for 6–8 hours. Cool, remove wet coverings. When cold, put on dry covers.
4 Steam for 2 hours on Christmas Day.
To prevent top of pudding becoming too wet, it is a good idea to make a flour and water paste. Mix about 8 oz. flour with enough water to make a firm dough, roll into a round the size of the top of the basin. Place this over greaseproof paper on the pudding, cover with more greaseproof paper and pudding is ready to cook.

New toppings for puddings (using the blender)

Apricot cream: Put 8 oz. raw apricots, 3 oz. sugar, juice of 1 lemon, and 1 oz. butter into blender. Switch on until smooth then put into basin and top with the sponge.

Apple ginger: Put 8 oz. (weight when peeled) dessert apples, juice of 1 orange, 2 oz. preserved ginger into blender. Switch on until smooth, then put into basin and top with the sponge.

Apple walnut: Substitute 2 oz. walnuts for the preserved ginger.

Tutti fruitti: Put 3 tablespoons apricot jam, juice 1 orange, 2 oz. glacé cherries, 2 oz. almonds into blender. Switch on until smooth. Put into basin and top with sponge.

More familiar toppings for sponge puddings

Jam, whole fresh fruit or well drained canned fruit or soaked and drained dried fruit, golden syrup, lemon curd, etc.

Puddings based on egg custards

These puddings must be cooked slowly, for the egg custard base could curdle and the pudding be spoiled.

Apricot macaroon pudding

cooking time	1½ hours
blender speed	medium

you will need for 4–6 servings:

3 eggs	2 medium-sized macaroon
1 oz. sugar	biscuits
1 pint milk	
6 oz. well drained canned apricots	
for the topping:	
½ oz. butter	2 oz. blanched almonds
about 8 apricot halves	
for the sauce:	
1 lemon	1 teaspoon cornflour or
syrup from can of apricots	arrowroot

1 Put the eggs, sugar, milk, apricots and macaroons into the blender.
2 Switch on until smoothly blended.
3 Allow to stand for any bubbles on top of the mixture to subside.

4 Meanwhile butter a 2-pint pudding basin. Put the apricots and nuts at the bottom then carefully spoon in the custard mixture.
5 Cover with buttered foil or greaseproof paper and steam over very hot but NOT boiling water until firm.
6 Turn out and serve hot with the sauce, made by blending the lemon juice with the syrup and cornflour and boiling until slightly thickened and clear.

Other fruit to use:
Dried apricots (soaked but not cooked), peaches, figs.

Lemon soufflé pudding

cooking time	45 minutes
mixer speed	low to medium then high

you will need for 4 servings:

2–3 oz. butter or margarine	2 eggs
3 oz. sugar	⅜ pint milk
grated rind and juice 2 good-sized lemons	**to decorate:**
2 oz. flour (with plain flour use ½ teaspoon baking powder)	lemon curd, pieces cherry and angelica

1 Put the butter or margarine and sugar into the mixing bowl and cream until soft and light.
2 Gradually beat in the lemon rind and juice, flour, egg yolks and milk; the mixture may curdle but this does not matter.
3 If you have only one bowl belonging to the mixer then transfer the mixture to a second bowl, wash the mixing bowl thoroughly, add the egg whites, switch to high speed and whisk until very stiff.
4 Fold the egg whites into the lemon mixture.
5 Pour into a greased pie dish or soufflé dish and stand this in another containing cold water.
6 Bake for about 45 minutes in the centre of a moderate oven (350–375°F.—Gas Mark 3–4).
7 Serve at once, brushed lightly with lemon curd and decorated with tiny pieces of cherry to make flowers and angelica leaves.

You will find the pudding separates—giving a soft sponge-like top layer and a curd sauce at the bottom. If preferred use oranges instead of lemons.

Variations:

Orange soufflé pudding: Use either all oranges (2 large ones) or 1½ oranges and ½ lemon for a better flavour.

Grapefruit soufflé pudding: Use a small grapefruit, but increase the sugar to 4 oz.

Chocolate soufflé pudding: Omit lemon rind and juice, add 2 oz. chocolate powder and nearly ½ pint milk.

Caramel crumb pudding

cooking time	1½ hours
blender speed	high then medium

you will need for 4–6 servings:

for the caramel:

3 oz. sugar	3 tablespoons water

for the pudding:

1 pint milk	3 eggs
1 tablespoon sherry	1–2 oz. sugar
2 oz. bread	4 oz. raisins
2–3 oz. walnuts or 1½ oz. walnuts and 1½ oz. blanched almonds	2 oz. glacé cherries

1 Make a caramel with the sugar and water; choose a strong saucepan, and stir over a low heat until the sugar has dissolved.
2 Boil steadily without stirring until a golden brown caramel. Pull the pan off the heat so the caramel cools slightly, this prevents the mixture curdling when the milk is added.
3 Pour in the milk and reheat over a low heat until the caramel and milk are well blended.
4 Add the sherry.
5 Put the bread and nuts into the dry blender goblet and switch on until finely chopped, then add the eggs and a little caramel liquid and switch on again for a few seconds until blended.
6 Tip out into a basin, add rest of the caramel mixture, the sugar, raisins and cherries.
7 Put into a well buttered 2-pint basin, cover with buttered foil or greaseproof paper and steam over very hot but NOT boiling water until firm.
8 Turn out and serve with cream or with brandy butter.

Coffee crumb pudding: This pudding is equally good if 2 tablespoons coffee essence are used instead of caramel.

Hot fruit soufflé

cooking time	45 minutes
blender speed	low then high
mixer speed	high

you will need for 4–5 servings:

approximately 12 oz. fruit (weight when prepared)	3–4 oz. sugar
very little water	3 eggs

to decorate:
little sieved icing sugar

1 Cook the fruit with enough water to prevent it burning in the pan, and sugar to taste.
2 Simmer until just tender, then put into the warmed blender goblet and switch gradually to high; when nearly smooth drop in the egg yolks and again switch on to blend.
3 Whisk the egg whites until very stiff, then gradually add the fruit purée.
4 Spoon into a greased soufflé dish and bake in the centre of a moderate to moderately hot oven (375–400°F.—Gas Mark 5), until just firm.
5 Top with icing sugar, and serve at once.
The most suitable fruits are: apricots, apples, blackcurrants, rhubarb, plums, etc.
The recipe above does not produce such a firm texture as the following recipe.

Hot soufflé

cooking time	40–45 minutes
mixer speed	high

½ oz. cornflour	1 oz. butter
¼ pint milk	2–3 oz. sugar (unless fruit already sweetened, then add extra sugar to taste)
2 tablespoons liqueur— brandy, Crème de Mênthe, etc., or use nearly ½ pint fruit purée and omit milk and liqueur	4 eggs

to decorate:
little sieved icing sugar

1 Blend the cornflour with the milk and put into a large saucepan and cook until thickened, stirring well, remove from the heat.
2 Stir in the liqueur, butter and sugar then the egg yolks.
3 Meanwhile whisk the egg whites until very stiff.
4 Fold into the hot soufflé mixture, then put into a buttered soufflé dish and bake for approximately 30–35 minutes in the centre of a moderate oven (350–375°F.—Gas Mark 4–5) until firm. Top with icing sugar and serve at once.

Speedy fruit amber

cooking time — 45 minutes
blender speed — low then high
mixer speed — high

you will need for 4 servings:

about ¾ pint fruit pulp
2 eggs
4 oz. sugar

1 oz. semi-sweet biscuits
  or sponge cake

1 Put the fruit, egg yolks, 2 oz. sugar and the biscuits or sponge into the blender.
2 Switch on until blended.
3 Pour or spoon into the pie dish.
4 Meanwhile whisk the egg whites until very stiff, and gradually add the sugar.
5 Pile the meringue over the fruit mixture and set for 45 minutes in a cool to very moderate oven (300–350°F.—Gas Mark 2–3).
6 Serve hot with cream or a sweet custard sauce.

Pastry making

A perfect pastry depends upon the correct balance of fat and flour, correct handling of the ingredients and keeping the ingredients as cool as possible.

A mixer is not of value in making the richer puff or flaky pastries, but it is invaluable for the 'rubbed-in' type, short crust, sweet short crust, etc., particularly in hot weather when one's hands are hot, for the metallic whisk, used at the correct speed, does not become over-heated.

Note:

When a recipe says 6 oz. pastry it means pastry made with 6 oz. flour, etc., NOT 6 oz. completed pastry.

Short crust pastry (with mixer)

cooking time — as recipe
mixer speed — low

ingredients as on right:

1 Put the flour, salt and the fat, cut into small pieces, into the mixing bowl. Never overfill the bowl or the flour will 'fly' in all directions.
2 Switch on the mixer to the very lowest speed and allow the blades to incorporate the fat into the flour.
3 Switch off and add the liquid by hand.
Never allow the mixer to over-handle pastry any more than you would over-handle it yourself.

Using the blender for pastry

Although this is not one of the main purposes, the blender (liquidiser) can be used for making short crust pastry or sweet short crust pastry. This is particularly valuable in hot weather when the fat tends to become sticky when handled with fingers.

Short crust pastry (with blender)

cooking time — as recipe
blender speed — medium then high

8 oz. flour, preferably
  plain
pinch salt

4 oz. fat
cold water to mix

1 Put the flour and salt into the DRY blender goblet. There is no need to sieve the flour.
2 Add the fat cut in small pieces; take care this does not stick to the sides of the goblet.
3 Switch gradually to medium then to high until evenly blended—do not leave running too long for the mixture could become sticky.
4 Tip into a bowl, add water to bind, and use as specific recipes.

Sweet short crust pastry

Recipe as above, but add ½–2 oz. sugar to the flour and salt. Bind with egg yolk and water, rather than all water.

Cheese pastry

Recipe as above, but use only 3½ oz. fat and 2 oz. cheese. Add liberal amount of seasoning to flour. Add fat and cheese together to the flour, unless the cheese is very fresh and sticky, when it is advisable to add the fat first. Switch off the motor, so the blender is not running for too long a period, then switch on again, adding the cheese in small cubes. Bind with egg yolk and water, rather than all water.

Biscuit crust pastry 1

blender speed	medium
mixer speed	low

4 oz. biscuits – these may be semi-sweet, sweet, ginger-nuts, digestive, etc., or use a mixture	2 oz. butter 1–2 oz. sugar ½ tablespoon golden syrup or honey (optional)

1 Put the biscuits into the dry blender goblet and switch on until fine crumbs.
2 Cream the butter and sugar with the mixer until soft – the golden syrup or honey gives a consistency that 'binds together' rather more readily.
3 Add the crumbs and allow the mixture to move slowly round until blended.
4 Form into flan shape. This need not be baked, but 10 minutes in a moderately hot oven gives additional crispness.
   Cornflake pastry: Use cornflakes instead of biscuits.
   Savoury biscuit crust: Use cheese flavoured biscuits, omit the sugar and syrup.

Biscuit crust pastry 2

This is the name given to the sweet short crust used for flans. It is also often called fleur pastry. Put 4–5 oz. butter with 2 oz. sugar into the mixer bowl, whisk on a low speed until soft. Switch off, add 8 oz. flour, sieved with a pinch of salt (preferably plain flour), and the yolk of an egg. Blend on the lowest possible speed. Stop the mixer and feel the consistency of the dough, gradually add, *by hand*, enough water to bind. Bake in a slightly cooler oven than for short crust pastry.

Time saving tip: Mix the fat and flour for pastry and keep it in a screw-topped jar or polythene bag in the refrigerator, ready for use.

Lemon chiffon pie

cooking time	25 minutes
juice extractor	medium
or juice separator	medium
mixer speed	low then high

you will need for 4–5 servings:

6 oz. short or sweet short crust pastry or use biscuit crust, see left

for the filling:

2 large lemons	1½ level dessertspoons powder gelatine
3 eggs	
3 oz. sugar	¼ pint thick cream
water	

1 Roll out the pastry and line an 8-inch flan ring, on an upturned baking sheet, or a pie dish or tin.
2 Fill with greaseproof paper and beans or crusts of bread and bake empty, i.e. 'blind' for approximately 20 minutes in a hot oven for short crust (425–450°F.—Gas Mark 6–7) or for approximately 25 minutes at a slightly lower temperature for sweet crust.
3 Extract the juice from the fruit with the juice extractor, having grated the rind very finely or choose loaf sugar and rub over the rind—a juice separator extracts so much flavour from the fruit that grating the rind is unnecessary.
4 Whisk egg yolks with the sugar and grated lemon rind until thick.
5 Measure lemon juice, add enough water to give ¼ pint, heat, dissolve gelatine in this, allow to cool.
6 Whip the cream on low speed, fold into lemon gelatine mixture and leave until just beginning to stiffen.
7 Whisk the egg whites on high speed and fold these into the half set lemon mixture.
8 Spoon into the pastry case and allow to set.

4 simple fillings for pastry cases

Coffee chiffon: Use recipe for lemon chiffon, but omit the lemon juice, use 2 tablespoons coffee essence made up to ¼ pint with water. Fold 2 oz. chopped nuts into the mixture when nearly set.

Jellied rhubarb: Dissolve a lemon jelly in ½ pint water, add ½ lb. sweetened cooked rhubarb, put into the blender, switch on until a smooth purée. Cool and allow to stiffen slightly, fold in ¼ pint lightly whipped cream then spoon into baked pastry cases, allow to set. Choose other fruits in season.

Lemon cream: Whip equal quantities of thick cream and lemon curd with the mixer.

Lemon meringue pie:
Extract juice from 2 lemons (see lemon chiffon pie). Add enough water to give ½ pint. Blend this with 1 oz. cornflour, put into saucepan with 1 oz. butter and 2–3 oz. sugar to taste, cook until thick. Add 2 egg yolks, continue cooking for 2–3 minutes without boiling. Put into lightly cooked pastry case. Whisk 2 egg whites until very stiff, gradually whisk in 2 oz. sugar (if serving hot) or 4 oz. sugar if serving cold. Either set for about 25 minutes in moderate oven (350–375°F.—Gas Mark 4) or about 1 hour in slow oven (250°F.—Gas Mark ½).

Savouries

There are many ways in which a mixer can save time when preparing savouries or savoury dishes, e.g. whisk the egg whites in soufflés; blend the cheese mixture in a Welsh rarebit, ensure a smooth sauce or sandwich filling.

With eggs

Savoury soufflés

cooking time	40 minutes
blender speed	medium
mixer speed	high

you will need for 4 people:

1 oz. butter	flavouring, see below
1 oz. flour	4 eggs, or 3 egg yolks and
¼ pint milk or other	4 egg whites
liquid	
seasoning	

1 Make a thick sauce with the butter, flour, and milk, add a little seasoning.

2 Put in the blender and add the flavouring, and egg yolks and switch to medium until well blended.

3 Whisk the egg whites in a large mixer bowl then gradually fold in the savoury mixture.

4 Put into a buttered soufflé dish and bake for approximately 30 minutes in a moderate to moderately hot oven (350–375°F.—Gas Mark 4–5). Serve at once.

Flavourings for soufflés

Cheese: Add 3 oz. cheese to the sauce.

Cheese and tomato: Use ¼ pint tomato juice or thin purée instead of milk and 3 oz. cheese.

Celery: Choose canned celery and use ¼ pint liquid and 2 heads celery, or 1 head celery and 2 oz. grated Parmesan cheese.

Ham: Add 4 oz. cooked ham to the mixture in the blender.

Fish: Use half fish stock and half thin cream for the liquid and add 4–6 oz. cooked fish to the mixture in the blender—white fish—shell fish—salmon, tuna, are all ideal fish to choose.

Scrambled eggs

The eggs and seasoning may be blended in the blender, but this is particularly useful when making a savoury scrambled egg. When the mixture is ready, scramble slowly in 1–2 oz. butter in a saucepan. 1–2 tablespoons milk or cream may be added to the egg mixture if wished.

allow 4–6 eggs for 3–4 people

Cheese: Put the eggs, seasoning and approximately 2–3 oz. cheese in the blender.

Ham: Put the eggs, pepper, little salt and 4 oz. cooked ham in the blender.

Piperade: Chop onion coarsely and fry in the hot butter in the pan, together with 2–3 skinned chopped tomatoes and 1 chopped green pepper. When lightly cooked tip into the blender goblet with the eggs and switch on briefly until the vegetables are chopped into medium-sized pieces and well blended.

Season well. Return to the pan, adding a little extra butter if wished and cook until just set.

Serve all scrambled eggs on hot buttered toast or fried bread.

With cheese

Welsh rarebit

This is a particularly soft and creamy mixture; so do not cover the edges of the hot toast, as it will tend to spread as cooked. There is no need to butter the toast.

cooking time	few minutes
blender speed	medium

you will need for 4 servings:*

for the rarebit:

3 tablespoons milk or use thin cream or half milk and half cream	shake black and cayenne pepper
1 tablespoon ale	1 teaspoon Worcestershire sauce
2 oz. butter	8 oz. Cheddar cheese
1 teaspoon made mustard	4 large slices bread
pinch salt	

to garnish:
2 tomatoes; parsley

*As a light meal or 8 servings for a savoury at the end of the meal.

1 Put all the rarebit ingredients into the blender, the butter should be softened and the cheese cut into pieces.
2 Switch on until blended, taste while in the blender and add extra seasoning if wished.
3 Remove from the blender at once, while the butter is still soft, this saves wasting any of the mixture round the blades.
4 Keep in a cool place until set.
5 Spread on the hot toast and put under the grill for a few minutes until brown.
6 Garnish with raw or grilled halved tomatoes and parsley.

Cheese choux pastry or cheese aigrettes

cooking time	10 minutes
mixer speed	medium

to make about 25 small savouries

1 oz. butter	2–3 eggs, see method, stage 5
¼ pint water	
seasoning	3 oz. grated Cheddar cheese
3 oz. flour	

to deep fry:
oil or fat

1 Put the butter, water and seasoning into a good-sized saucepan.
2 Heat until the butter has melted, then remove the pan from the heat and gradually beat in the flour.
3 Return to the heat and blend well with the whisk (over a very gentle heat) until the mixture forms a dry ball.
4 Again remove the mixture from the heat; if you have no portable mixer then proceed as above without using the mixer, then transfer to the mixing bowl.
5 Beat the eggs in gradually, you will probably find you need 2 whole eggs and the yolk of the third, but the mixture should be a *sticky* consistency.
6 Stir in the cheese.
7 Heat the oil or fat, see testing method, page 22, but as these take a minute or so longer in cooking the bread should turn golden in 1 minute or ½ minute with oil.

8 Drop small spoonfuls of the mixture into the fat or oil, or put into a piping bag with $\frac{1}{2}$ inch plain pipe and press mixture through this. Cook until crisp and golden brown, drain on absorbent paper, and serve tossed in grated cheese.

Cheese and nut aigrettes

Add 2 oz. finely chopped nuts (do this in the blender) to the mixture.

Baked cheese choux

1 Make the mixture as the cheese aigrettes but omit the cheese in the recipe.
2 Pipe small balls of the mixture on well greased baking trays.
3 Bake for approximately 15 minutes in the centre of a hot oven (425–450°F.—Gas Mark 7–8) until golden brown.
4 Allow to cool.
5 Blend the cheese with $\frac{1}{4}$ pint whipped cream and seasoning, split the choux buns and fill.

Sandwich fillings

Before preparing these read the remarks on page 13 about pâtés, for sandwich fillings should be a similar consistency and the problems are the same.

As a high percentage of butter is used in the fillings (to help emulsify the mixture) then extra butter on the bread could be omitted if wished.

All recipes give enough to fill about 6 rounds (large sized sandwich loaf).

The mixture is put into the blender and left until the desired consistency—with smaller models you will need to do part of the mixture then repeat the process (there is no need to wash the goblet between).

Cheese spreads

1 5 oz. Cheddar cheese, 2 oz. melted butter, 1 tablespoon thick cream, 2 hard-boiled eggs and seasoning (including few drops Worcestershire sauce and made mustard to taste).
2 3 oz. cream cheese, 3 oz. Cheddar or Gruyère or Parmesan cheese, 1 oz. melted butter, seasoning.
3 As numbers 1 or 2 but add 2 skinned tomatoes.
4 As numbers 1 or 2 with a small bunch watercress (leaves only) and a little chutney.

Egg spreads

1 2 teaspoons horseradish cream, 4–5 hard boiled eggs, 2 oz. melted butter, 2 tablespoons mayonnaise, seasoning.
2 As number 1 but add 2 skinned tomatoes and omit horseradish.
3 4 hard boiled eggs, 2 tablespoons mayonnaise, 1 oz. melted butter, $\frac{1}{2}$ green pepper, small sprig parsley, 1 tablespoon thick cream.

Fish spreads

1 Medium can salmon (minus liquid in the can), small pieces of peeled cucumber, 2 tablespoons mayonnaise, 1 oz. melted butter.
2 3 oz. melted butter, medium can salmon (minus any juice) or 4 oz. melted butter, 8–10 oz. cooked salmon and seasoning to taste.
3 Use tuna fish in place of salmon.
4 8 oz. flaked smoked haddock, 2 hard boiled eggs, 2 oz. melted butter, 1 tablespoon mayonnaise.

Meat spreads

1 6 oz. diced cooked ham, 2 oz. butter, 2 teaspoons made mustard, 1 tablespoon thick cream.
2 As above, but omit the cream and add 2 medium skinned tomatoes.

Using a blender for omelettes and batters

The blender is extremely useful to blend the eggs, etc., for an omelette or the batter for pancakes or a Yorkshire pudding.

Note the remark about the order of adding the flour for pancakes on page 71.

Omelettes

Omelette aux fines herbes

Put the required number of eggs, seasoning and a small bunch of mixed fresh herbs into the goblet. Switch gradually to high speed for a very short time.

Cheese omelette

If adding cheese when the omelette is partially cooked, this should be prepared in the blender goblet separately. See page 10.

You can, however, make a very delicious omelette with the cheese added to the eggs. To 3 eggs (enough for 2 people) put 1½–2 oz. cheese cut in small pieces. Add seasoning. Switch the blender gradually to high until the cheese is blended with the egg. Take great care not to over-cook this particular omelette otherwise the cheese becomes tough.

Ham omelette

Put the eggs and seasoning into the blender goblet. Switch on for approximately 30 seconds, then add desired amount of ham, proportions as for cheese. Leave for a short time only, so the ham remains in definite pieces.

Mushroom omelette

Fry 2 oz. mushrooms in 1 oz. butter.
Put 3 eggs, seasoning and the fried mushrooms into the goblet, switch on for a short time only.

Spanish omelette

Recipes for this are varied.
Some Spanish omelettes are made with onion and potato only, others from mixed vegetables, and it is in this type of omelette that the blender saves time chopping vegetables finely. Fry half a diced green pepper, one sliced onion in 1 oz. butter. Add 2 *halved* tomatoes and cook for a very short time only.

Put 4–5 eggs, seasoning, into the goblet, switch to high for a few seconds only, then tip in the vegetables and switch on until they are made into finely chopped pieces.

To cook an omelette

Heat at least 1 oz. butter in the omelette pan. Pour in the egg mixture, cook quickly until set on the bottom, move the liquid egg away from the sides of the pan, at the same time tipping the pan so the top liquid egg flows underneath. Continue like this until cooked. Fold omelette—except for a Spanish omelette which is served flat.

Note:

Soufflé omelettes cannot be prepared in the blender.

Soufflé omelette

Choose the same amount of eggs as for a plain omelette, but separate the yolks and the whites. Put the yolks in one bowl, add seasoning for a savoury omelette or a little sugar to taste for a sweet omelette (approximately 1 oz. to 3 eggs). Whisk these—a teaspoon water, milk or cream to each yolk may be added. Meanwhile whisk the egg whites in the mixing bowl until very stiff, fold into the egg yolks. Heat 1 oz. butter in the omelette pan, pour in the omelette mixture and cook gently until the eggs are set on the bottom. This very thick omelette will not cook through as a plain omelette so put the pan under a hot grill and set the eggs until pale golden. Put in the filling: savoury fillings can be cheese sauce, chicken in sauce, etc. Sweet fillings can be jam, ice cream, fruit, etc. Make a definite cut in the omelette to encourage it to fold. Fold over and serve. Sprinkle sieved icing sugar on top of a sweet omelette if wished, mark in a design with a skewer and put under the hot grill to caramelise.

Batter for pancakes and Yorkshire pudding

cooking time   as recipe
blender speed   high

you will need for 4 servings:

½ pint milk OR   4 oz. flour (preferably
  milk and water   plain)
1 egg   pinch salt

1 In order to prevent any flour being wasted round the sides of the goblet, put the liquid and egg into the goblet first.
2 Put in the flour and salt.
3 Switch GRADUALLY to high speed and leave until blended.

To cook pancakes

Heat enough oil or fat in a pan to give a very thin coating. Pour in enough batter to cover the bottom of the pan. Cook quickly, then toss or turn and cook on the second side. Fold or roll.
Sweet pancakes are served with lemon and sugar; filled with jam or fruit; ice cream (at the last minute), etc.
Savoury pancakes are filled with meat or fish in a sauce; cheese and vegetables in a sauce, etc.

To make a Yorkshire pudding

Heat a good knob of fat in a Yorkshire pudding tin. Pour in the batter and cook for approximately 35 minutes in a very hot oven, reducing the heat after 10 to 15 minutes if necessary.

A plain, savoury Yorkshire pudding is the traditional accompaniment to beef

Variations on this are:

Toad-in-the-hole: Heat approximately 1 lb. sausages with the fat for 5–10 minutes. Pour over the batter, recipe above, and cook as Yorkshire pudding.
Cheese batter: Add 3 oz. cheese to the blender goblet when making the batter. Cook as Yorkshire pudding, top with cooked vegetables for a light supper dish.

Sweet baked batters

Norfolk pudding: Heat 1 oz. butter and approximately 12 oz. peeled, sliced, cooking apples for 10 minutes. Add 2–3 oz. dried fruit, and 1 oz. sugar to the Yorkshire pudding batter, opposite. Pour over the hot apples, top with powdered spice and bake as Yorkshire pudding.

Orange or lemon batters: Mix the batter with lemon juice or orange juice and water in place of milk. A little fruit rind may also be added to the batter in the blender. Bake as Yorkshire pudding and serve hot with marmalade as a quick dessert.

Coating batter for fritters

cooking time   as recipe
blender speed   high

you will need for 4 servings:

¼–½ pint milk and   4 oz. flour—plain or
  water (depending on the   self-raising
  food to be coated)   seasoning
1 egg

1 In order to prevent any flour being wasted round the sides of the goblet put the liquid and egg into the goblet first.
2 Put in the flour and salt, etc.
3 Switch GRADUALLY to high speed and leave until blended.

To cook fritters

Savoury fritters

Coat pieces of cooked meat, lightly cooked cauliflower florets (rather large sprigs), segments of processed cheese, etc., with the batter. Fry in really hot fat or oil until crisp and golden. Drain on absorbent paper.

Sweet fritters

Dip rings of peeled, cored apples, ¼–½ inch in thickness, in flour and then in batter, or use rings of well-drained canned pineapple, or small bananas. Fry until crisp and brown, drain on absorbent paper and roll in sugar.

Cake-making with a mixer

Many of you will have purchased a mixer chiefly for preparing the ingredients of a cake and this will save a great deal of physical effort as well as producing excellent results if the right technique is followed. Read the comments on page 7 and below, also the advice given in the manufacturer's book.

Use of a mixer in cake-making

Action	Used for	Choice of attachment where available	Speed to use	Flour to be added
Whisking	eggs and sugar for sponges, egg whites and sugar for meringues	whisk	high	by hand
Creaming	fat and sugar for Victoria sandwich, cherry cakes, fruit cakes, etc.	K beater	low to medium	by hand
Rubbing in	fat into flour for plain cakes	whisk or K beater whichever preferred	low	on low speed by machine
Beating	for melted mixtures such as gingerbread	whisk or K beater whichever preferred	medium	on low speed by machine
Kneading	yeast doughs	dough hook	low	on low speed by machine

Where there is no choice of attachment then use the whisk provided with the mixer but try to adjust the speed.

Creaming method: Warm the bowl before putting the fat and sugar in, so they cream easily. DO NOT melt the fat as this will prevent the cake being light.

Cakes made by whisking method

Make sure the eggs are at room temperature. Use castor sugar in this type of cake.
Keep flour in a warm place after sieving.
When you adapt the directions for any cake check that you are following the right procedure for that type of cake.

Important
Read the notes in the recipes and on page 7 about adding the flour. Many cakes are spoiled in texture because the flour is added too vigorously.

Use of blender for cake making

The blender (liquidiser) is not specifically designed for making cakes. It can, however, be utilised for blending commercial packets of cake mixes, and also for quick sponges although the texture is not as good as if the eggs and sugar were whisked properly as on right.

Sponge cake

cooking time   20–25 minutes. See Stage 6
mixer speed   high

you need for 5–6 portions:

2 large eggs   1 dessertspoon hot water
2–3 oz. castor sugar

2 oz. flour (plain or   **to coat tin:**
    self-raising flour)   little butter
                       shaking of flour or flour
                         and castor sugar

1 Put the eggs and sugar into a large mixing bowl, switch on and whisk until the mixture is thick and creamy (you see the trail of the whisk). If you have a portable mixer then you can put the bowl over a saucepan or larger bowl of hot water—this makes sure the eggs whisk up more quickly but care must be taken they do not set round the edges of the bowl. If whisking over hot water allow mixture to cool BEFORE adding the flour.

2 Sieve the flour at least once.

3 Fold gently into the egg mixture with a metal spoon—lastly fold in the water. If you like to use a very low speed for this you may, but it is better to do this by hand for over-beating of the flour at this stage is the biggest reason for failure in this kind of cake.

4 Grease and flour a 6 or 7 inch cake tin lightly, then coat with flour or an equal mixture of flour and castor sugar.

5 Spoon mixture carefully into tin.

6 Bake in the centre of the oven—use a moderate temperature, approximately 350–375°F.—Gas Mark 4–5, for the sponge must not brown too quickly—and you may need to reduce the heat very slightly after about 10 minutes. A 6 inch cake should take about 25 minutes but a 7 inch cake will cook a little more quickly.

7 Test cake before removing from oven—press with finger, if no impression remains the cake is cooked.

8 Turn the cake out carefully, allowing it 1 minute to cool in tin.

9 This can either be served quite plain, topping with sieved icing sugar or castor sugar if wished or split and filled with jam, jam and cream or butter icing, see page 81.

Sponge sandwich

Use the recipe, left, and bake in two 6–7 inch sandwich tins allowing approximately 8–9 minutes towards the top of a moderately hot oven (375–400°F.—Gas Mark 5–6).

Swiss roll

Use recipe, left, but make sure the mixture is soft, increase water if necessary and *pour* into a small Swiss roll tin, lined with greased greaseproof paper and bake for approximately 7–9 minutes in a moderately hot oven. Test with particular care as over-baking causes cake to break. Turn the cake on to sugared paper, cut away any crisp edges and spread with warmed jam. Make a light cut at one end of the sponge to help make the first fold, then roll away from you. If filling with whipped cream or butter cream, roll round greaseproof paper; when quite cold, un-roll and spread with the filling and roll gently and carefully once again.

Sponge flan

The mixture can be baked in a greased and floured flan tin—2 eggs, etc., is sufficient for a 9 inch flan tin. This will take approximately 12 minutes towards the top of a moderately hot oven (375°F.—Gas Mark 5). Turn out and fill with fruit, etc., when the sponge is quite cold.

Continental nut gâteau

Use the same recipe as for sponge cake, above left, but omit the flour completely. Instead use 2 oz. nuts—these can be ground almonds and to be authentic they should be ground with their skins to give more flavour to the cake or use ground hazel nuts (use the blender for this) or they can be purchased in good stores.

Make the cake and bake as the sponge cake, sponge sandwich or the Swiss roll. Fill when cold with whipped cream or butter cream. If your tins are inclined to make cakes stick then line with greased and floured greaseproof paper instead of just coating the tins as suggested when using flour.

Continental crumb gâteau

Use the same recipe as for sponge cake, see page 73, but omit the flour and instead use crisp, very fine breadcrumbs. These can be crumbs made from toasted bread and put into the blender goblet to make them very fine. Make the cake and bake as the sponge cake or sponge sandwich; as the mixture is slightly brittle it is less suitable for a Swiss roll. It is advisable to line the tin or tins with greased and floured paper for this cake mixture.

Angel cake

This American cake with its light, fine texture makes a complete change and is very easy with a mixer. Read remarks about whisking egg whites on page 52.

Put 6 large or 8 smaller egg whites into the mixing bowl and whisk on high speed until very stiff. Sieve 4 oz. flour (plain or self-raising, but preferably the former) with $\frac{1}{2}$ teaspoon cream of tartar. Fold 6 oz. castor sugar, then the flour, into the egg whites, lastly fold in few drops vanilla essence. Butter an angel tin, i.e. a ring mould, and put in mixture. Bake for just 1 hour, if using a tin measuring 8–9 inches in diameter, in a slow oven (250–300°F.—Gas Mark 1). Do not turn cake out of tin straight away, but turn upside-down over a wire sieve and it should drop from tin when cold.

If egg whites are very fresh and therefore whip up to very dry mixture, fold 1 tablespoon water into mixture at end. This gives softer texture. When cake is cold, cover with water icing, decorate with cherries.

Quick sponge

cooking time	10–12 minutes
blender speed	medium

to give 6 portions you need:

2 eggs	2 oz. self-raising flour
2–3 oz. sugar	a little jam

1 Put the eggs and sugar into the blender goblet, switch gradually to a medium speed and leave for about one minute until the mixture is very frothy looking.
2 Add the flour and leave the blender switched on until it is blended – when adding the flour try to avoid putting this round the edge of the goblet (in case any sticks).
3 Grease and flour two 6-inch tins, divide the mixture between these tins and bake until firm to the touch towards the top of a moderately hot oven (375–400°F.—Gas Mark 5–6). When cool sandwich together with a little jam.

Japonnaise cakes

cooking time	45–50 minutes
mixer speed	high then low

you will need for about 8 cakes:

4 egg whites	few drops almond or
8 oz. sugar	ratafia essence
8 oz. ground almonds or	
use 8 oz. blanched	
almonds and grind these in	
the blender, see page 10	

to decorate:

4 oz. butter	$\frac{1}{2}$–1 tablespoon coffee
6 oz. sieved icing	essence
sugar	8 hazel nuts

1 Put egg whites into bowl, switch on and whisk on high speed until stiff.
2 Reduce speed to low and gradually whisk in half the sugar, fold in the remainder with ground almonds and essence.
3 Grease and flour a deep baking tin or line a more shallow tin with greased greaseproof paper or foil to support the cake mixture during cooking.
4 Bake mixture for about 30 minutes in centre of a slow to very moderate oven (300–325°F.—Gas Mark 2–3) until almost set, remove from oven.
5 Cut about 16 small rounds then return to oven for further 10 minutes or until quite firm.
6 Remove once more from oven, lift out rounds of cake, allow these to cool.
7 Return 'trimmings' to oven for further 10 minutes or until very brown and crisp.
8 Crush 'trimmings' with rolling pin or put into blender goblet, switch to medium or low speed until fine crumbs.
9 Blend butter and icing sugar with mixer on low speed, then gradually add coffee essence.
10 Sandwich the rounds with a little of this mixture, coat cakes then roll in the crumbs.
11 Complete with a piped rosette of coffee butter icing on top and a hazel nut.

Coffee Japonnaise cakes: As recipe above, but add 2 teaspoons instant coffee to the sugar.

Chocolate Japonnaise cakes: Add 1 oz. sieved cocoa or 2 oz. chocolate powder to sugar, together with a few drops water to give softer texture. Coat with chocolate butter icing instead of coffee if wished.

Meringues

cooking time   2–4 hours (depending on size)
mixer speed   high then low

you will need for 6 large meringues when sandwiched together or about 24 small meringues or fingers

2 egg whites	very little butter or oil for
4 oz. castor sugar OR	greasing tin
2 oz. castor sugar and	**to fill:**
2 oz. sieved icing	whipped cream or butter
sugar	cream, see page 81

1 Whisk the egg whites until very stiff—it is important that they are 24 hours old (a new egg white will NOT whip stiffly) and that they are whisked in a clean container—a speck of yolk or smear of grease could prevent their becoming stiff. A high speed can be used for this stage.
2 Have the sugar ready by the mixer bowl.
3 Reduce the speed of the mixer to low, then gradually add the sugar—do not put this in too quickly—see comments on page 52.
4 Oil or butter baking tray lightly, then spoon on the meringue mixture or put into a bag with a large pipe—make 12 equal-sized rounds or 24 small rounds or fingers.
5 Bake until hard—tiny meringues will take about 2 hours, really large ones about $3\frac{1}{2}$–4 hours, preferably in the coolest part of a very cool oven—this varies between 225–250°F.—Gas Mark $\frac{1}{4}$–1.
6 Remove from the tin by lifting with a warmed palette knife, cool thoroughly.
7 When cold, store in an airtight tin until ready to fill.
8 Sandwich together with whipped cream or butter cream.
Meringues Chantilly: Add a little vanilla essence and sugar to the whipped cream used to sandwich the meringues.
Meringues glacés: Sandwich together with ice cream and decorate with whipped cream if wished.

Victoria sandwich

cooking time   20 minutes
mixer speed   low to medium

you need for 6 portions:

4 oz. margarine or butter	4 oz. self-raising flour (or
4 oz. castor sugar	plain flour and 1 level
2 large eggs	teaspoon baking powder)

filling:	**decoration:**
3 tablespoons jam	castor or sieved icing sugar

1 Put the margarine or butter into the bowl with the sugar. Read comments on page 72 about warming the bowl, before creaming a mixture.
2 Switch to low speed until the mixture begins to soften then the speed can be increased but if using too high a speed the mixture may splash outside the bowl or will be flung against the sides of the bowl, and time will be wasted scraping this down.
If using a hand mixer keep this moving well round the bowl, so that ALL the mixture is evenly creamed.
3 Whisk the eggs in a basin, then add gradually to the creamed fat and sugar. **Remember a mixture curdles just as readily when blended with a mixer as when blended by hand.** If the mixture shows signs of curdling add a little sieved flour.
4 Fold in sieved flour with a metal spoon, taking care not to overhandle—read comments on page 7 about adding flour to cake mixtures.
5 Bake for approximately 20 minutes about 2 rungs from the top of the oven, or in an electric oven you may be able to bake the cakes either towards the top or the bottom of the oven—read your own cooker manufacturer's instructions. The ideal temperature for a Victoria sandwich varies with individual cookers, generally you need a moderate oven (350–375°F.—Gas Mark 4–5).
6 Test cakes before removing from oven—press gently with finger, if no impression remains cake is cooked.
7 Cool on a wire cooling tray, sandwich with jam, top with sugar.

Coffee sponge: Use 2 small eggs and add 1 tablespoon coffee essence to these.
Chocolate sponge: Use 3 oz. flour and 1 oz. chocolate powder, or $3\frac{1}{2}$ oz. flour and $\frac{1}{2}$ oz. cocoa.

Cherry cake

cooking time	$1\frac{1}{4}$–$1\frac{1}{2}$ hours
mixer speed	low to medium

you need for 8–10 portions:

4 oz. butter or margarine	6 oz. plain flour
4 oz. castor sugar	1 level teaspoon baking
2 eggs	powder
few drops of vanilla	3–4 oz. glacé cherries
essence	$1\frac{1}{2}$ tablespoons milk

1 Put the butter or margarine into the bowl with the sugar. Read comments on page 72 about warming the bowl before creaming the mixture.
2 See point 2 under Victoria sandwich.
3 See point 3 under Victoria sandwich.
4 Fold in the vanilla essence and the sieved flour and baking powder with a metal spoon, read comments on page 7 about adding flour to cake mixtures.
5 Add the cherries—these should be halved or quartered and coated in flour. If very sticky they should be rinsed in cold water then dried to prevent their sinking; then add milk.
6 Put into a greased and floured 6–7 inch cake tin, level the top.
7 Bake for time given, in the centre of a very moderate oven (300–350°F.—Gas Mark 3–4).
8 Test cake before removing from tin—ensure the cake has shrunk away from the sides of the tin and feels firm to the touch.

Caraway seed cake: As cherry cake but use self-raising flour, omit the cherries and add 2–3 teaspoons caraway seeds, top the cake with sugar and a light sprinkling of seeds before baking.
Date cake: Use chopped dates instead of cherries, self-raising flour instead of plain flour.
Dundee cake: As cherry cake but use 12 oz. dried fruit, same amount of baking powder and plain flour is ideal. Top with 1–2 oz. blanched almonds before baking.

One-stage cakes

With the development of quick creaming margarine and cooking fat, it is now possible to make cakes by a far quicker method than in the past.

To do this you must choose a margarine or cooking fat that is classified as 'quick creaming'—various other words are used . . . 'luxury' margarine, etc.

A Victoria sandwich is given as an example of this, but most cakes can be made by this method, except very special cakes (see the disadvantages below).

The advantage is:
The cake is prepared in a matter of 2–3 minutes (when once the ingredients are weighed, etc.).

The disadvantages are:
1 The cake does not rise as well as when the usual creaming method is followed, unless extra baking powder is used—although the vigorous action of an electric mixer incorporates more air than a short hand mixing.
2 The cake does not keep as well, particularly if the extra baking powder is used to make the cake rise. To make the cake keep is naturally less important in a family where the cake *is* eaten when fresh.

Victoria sandwich by the one-stage method

cooking time	as Victoria sandwich page 75
mixer speed	low to medium

you need for 6 portions:

4 oz. quick-creaming margarine (cooking fat could be used)	4 oz. self-raising flour, plus generous $\frac{1}{2}$ level teaspoon baking powder or plain
4 oz. castor sugar	flour and $1\frac{1}{2}$ level tea-
2 large eggs	spoons baking powder

1 Put all the ingredients into the mixing bowl. Read comments on page 72 about warming the bowl, but most of these margarines and fats NEVER harden even when kept in a refrigerator.
2 Switch on until blended – this will take about 2 minutes.
3 Continue as from stage 5 for the Victoria sandwich page 75.
The blender could be used in an emergency (where no mixer is available) to blend this cake if the fat is melted, but the results ARE NOT particularly good.

Economical 'Cut and come again' cake

cooking time   1–1¼ hours
mixer speed   low

you will need for 8–10 portions:

8 oz. self-raising flour (or plain flour and 2 level teaspoons baking powder)	3–4 oz. sugar
	4 oz. currants
	4 oz. sultanas
1 level teaspoon mixed spice	1 oz. mixed peel
	1 egg
½ level teaspoon cinnamon	approximately ¼ pint milk
3–4 oz. butter, margarine or cooking fat or well clarified dripping	

1 Sieve the flour or flour and baking powder with spice and cinnamon into the mixer bowl, or a mixing bowl sufficiently large for the movement of the whisk.

2 Add the butter or other fat and switch on to blend the ingredients together – where mixers have a high speed you must use a very large bowl so that the flour does not 'fly' in all directions.

3 Add the sugar, dried fruit and peel, do this by hand as mixing is unnecessary at this stage.

4 Mix with eggs and milk to form a soft consistency, i.e. so the mixture drops easily from a knife – a mixer could be used but as the mixture is rather sticky you are likely to waste some on the whisk.

5 Put into either a greased and floured 2 lb. loaf tin or 7-inch round tin, making the mixture quite level on top.

6 Bake in the centre of a moderate oven, 350–375°F.—Gas Mark 4 is the usual temperature. Allow approximately 1 hour for the loaf tin, the cake in the round tin may take a little longer.

7 Check that the cake has shrunk away from sides of the tin before bringing it out of the oven, then test by pressing firmly or with a fine skewer.

8 This cake should be eaten when reasonably fresh.

Apple cake: Ingredients as above, but use 4 oz. dried fruit only and 1 diced fairly sweet type cooking apple. Add this before the milk as you will not need quite so much since the apple provides juicy texture.

Date: Use dates (cut into neat pieces) or dates and walnuts instead of other dried fruit.

Chocolate: Use 7 oz. flour and 1 oz. cocoa for a chocolate-flavoured fruit cake.

Note:

If you have a blender but no mixer read the comments on page 72 about 'rubbing in' method with this.

The melting method: In this method the fat, etc., are melted in a saucepan then the dry ingredients added.

If using a portable mixer then choose a large saucepan and blend together in this.

If using a non-portable mixer put the flour, etc., into a large mixing bowl or the bowl belonging to the mixer, then pour the melted ingredients into this.

Gingerbread

cooking time   1–1¼ hours
mixer speed   low

you will need for 10–12 portions:

4 oz. butter, margarine or cooking fat	½ level teaspoon bicarbonate of soda
5 oz. black treacle	2 teaspoons powered ginger
2 oz. golden syrup	
5 oz. brown sugar	2 eggs
8 oz. self-raising flour or plain flour with 1½ level teaspoons baking powder	2 tablespoons water

1 Put the butter, treacle, syrup and sugar into the saucepan; heat steadily until the butter has melted.

2 Sieve the dry ingredients together, then either beat these into the melted ingredients or pour the melted ingredients on to the flour, etc., then add the eggs and water (see notes above the recipe).

3 Pour into an 8-inch square tin or Yorkshire pudding tin lined with greased greaseproof paper and bake for approximately 1¼ hours in the centre of a very moderate oven (300–350°F.—Gas Mark 3). Test by pressing gently and cool away from a draught.

Golden gingerbread: Use all golden syrup and omit the treacle.

Honey gingerbread: Use honey in place of golden syrup and flavour with grated rind of 1 lemon.

Fruit gingerbread: Add 4 oz. dried fruit and 2 oz. chopped nuts.

Orange cake: Use marmalade in place of golden syrup and treacle and flavour with grated rind of 1 orange – use 2 tablespoons orange juice in place of water.

Bread making

Most yeast or other bread doughs entail quite an amount of physical effort in kneading the dough. This can be avoided by using a mixer.

A dough hook with its slow careful movement is ideal, but as you will see on the table on page 72 a whisk could be used, but it is important that your mixer gives a slow steady speed for handling the dough.

This page gives one basic dough for yeast bread and a basic bun dough, but all your own recipes can be used if you follow the same technique.

Bread

cooking time   see method
mixer speed   low

you will need for a large loaf:

1 lb. plain flour (strong flour is ideal)	1 teaspoon sugar
$\frac{1}{2}$–1 teaspoon salt (little more if wished)	approximately $\frac{1}{2}$ pint tepid water
$\frac{1}{2}$ oz. yeast or $\frac{1}{2}$ level teaspoon dried yeast	

1 Sieve the flour and salt into the mixing bowl.
2 If using fresh yeast cream with the sugar and add the tepid liquid and a sprinkling of flour (use just under $\frac{1}{2}$ pint liquid). If using dried yeast dissolve the sugar in the tepid liquid, sprinkle the yeast on top, stand for 10 minutes, blend, sprinkle with flour and proceed as for fresh yeast.
3 Leave the yeast liquid until the top is covered with bubbles then pour on to the flour.
4 MIX SLOWLY AND CAREFULLY until a smooth soft dough, add little extra tepid water if needed.
5 Cover the bowl with a sheet of polythene or a clean cloth and leave in a warm place until the dough doubles. This takes about 1 hour.
6 Knead again, to test if sufficiently kneaded press with your finger and if the impression comes out the bread is ready.
7 Form into the required shape, for a tin loaf grease and warm a 2 lb. loaf tin and put in the bread.
8 Leave in a warm place to 'prove', i.e. rise for approximately 20 minutes until about one third the original size.
9 Bake in the centre of a hot to very hot oven (425–450°F.—Gas Mark 7–8), for 15 minutes then lower the heat to moderately hot (400°F.—Gas Mark 5–6), for a further 20–25 minutes until golden brown. To test if cooked remove from the tin with a clean cloth, knock on the bottom and the loaf should sound hollow.

A long shaped loaf will take about 25–30 minutes cooking time; a round 'cob' loaf about the same time.

Milk loaf: use milk instead of water and rub 1 oz. butter into flour.

Brown bread: use half wholemeal and half white flour; you may need a little extra liquid.

Yeast bun dough

cooking time   12–15 minutes
mixer speed   low

you will need for about 12 buns:

12 oz. plain flour	$\frac{1}{2}$ oz. yeast or $1\frac{1}{2}$ level teaspoons dried yeast
good pinch salt	
1–2 oz. butter or margarine	just over $\frac{1}{4}$ pint tepid milk or milk and water
2–3 oz. sugar	

1 Sieve the flour and salt, add the butter and switch on the mixer until the butter is 'rubbed in'. Add most of the sugar, but save about 1 teaspoon.
2 As stage 2 for the bread then continue as the bread until stage 7.
3 Form into required shapes, see below, and put on to warmed greased baking sheets, allowing room for the buns to spread out as well as rise.
4 Leave in a warm place for approximately 15 minutes then bake just above the centre of a hot to very hot oven (425–450°F.—Gas Mark 7–8) until firm to the touch.

Swiss buns: Form into finger shapes. Bake then when cold cover with glacé icing.

Fruit buns: Add 3–4 oz. dried fruit. Bake, and while still warm brush the tops with a glaze made by blending 2 tablespoons water and 2 tablespoons sugar.

Doughnuts: Form into balls, allow to 'prove' then fry steadily in very hot fat, drain on absorbent paper and roll in sugar. Split and fill with jam and whipped cream or make a 'hole' in the dough before 'proving' and put in jam, re-roll and 'prove' then fry.

Biscuits and small cakes

Many biscuits and small cakes may be prepared with the mixer or blender (liquidiser), but biscuit dough is often so firm that the mixer may experience difficulty in the final stages.

Honey crisps

cooking time	15 minutes
mixer speed	low to medium

you will need for 12 balls:

3 oz. butter or margarine	grated rind 1 lemon
1 oz. sugar	5 oz. self-raising flour
2 level tablespoons honey	

to decorate:

6 oz. icing sugar	lemon juice
2 teaspoons honey	

1 Put the butter, sugar and honey into a mixing bowl, together with the lemon rind.
2 Switch to low speed until well mixed.
3 Add the flour and continue mixing together.
4 Remove from bowl, form into balls and put on lightly greased baking trays or sheets—allowing room for the mixture to flatten and spread in cooking.
5 Bake near the centre of a moderate oven (350–375°F.—Gas Mark 4–5) until golden.
6 Cool on tin—store until ready to serve then top with icing made by blending the sieved icing sugar, honey and lemon juice.

Coconut bars

cooking time	20 minutes
mixer speed	high then low
blender speed	high

you will need for 12–14 biscuits

6 oz. desiccated coconut	2 large egg whites
2 oz. walnuts or hazel nuts	1 level tablespoon corn-flour
2 oz. glacé cherries	4 oz. sugar

1 Put the coconut and nuts into the goblet and switch on until fairly finely chopped. Cut the cherries into pieces.

2 Put the egg whites into the mixer bowl. Switch to high until lightly whisked, they should not be stiff.
3 Leave mixer running and gradually add the cornflour, sugar, coconut, nuts and cherries.
4 Form into finger shapes (with slightly damp hands) on rice paper or a well greased tin.
5 Bake for approximately 15–20 minutes until very pale golden, near centre of a moderate oven (350–375°F.—Gas Mark 4–5).
6 Cool slightly then remove from tin or tear round rice paper. If wished these may be coated with melted chocolate.

Almond fingers: Use ground almonds in place of coconut. Use blanched almonds in place of hazel nuts or walnuts.

Shortcake

Although this is NOT a true biscuit, its texture is a combination of sponge and biscuit—because it is well kneaded it is ideal for preparing with the help of a mixer.

cooking time	20 minutes
mixer speed	low

you will need for 8 servings:

for the shortcake:

4 oz. butter or margarine	2 medium eggs
4 oz. sugar	6 oz. self-raising flour

to fill and decorate:

$\frac{1}{4}$ to $\frac{1}{3}$ pint thick cream	12 oz.–1 lb. fresh or well-drained canned fruit

1 Put the butter and sugar into the bowl, switch the mixer to low speed until well blended.
2 Gradually add the eggs.
3 Add the flour and leave until well blended. DO NOT add liquid.
4 Grease and flour two 7 inch sandwich tins, divide the mixture in half, roll or pat out to 7 inch rounds and put in the tins.
5 Bake for approximately 20 minutes, above the centre of a very moderate to moderate oven (300–375°F.—Gas Mark 3–4) until firm.
6 Turn out very carefully and cool.
7 Sandwich together with whipped cream and fruit and top with whipped cream and fruit.

Small cakes: Many small cakes may be prepared from the basic recipes given.

Fairy cakes: Use Victoria sandwich recipe, add 4 oz. currants.

Queen cakes: Use Victoria sandwich recipe but 3 oz. butter and 3 oz. sugar.

Bake these cakes towards top of a moderately hot to hot oven (375–400°F.—Gas Mark 5–6) for 15 minutes.

The basic Queen Cake mixture may be turned into:

Butterfly cakes: Cook and when cold remove the tops, fill cakes with jam and whipped cream, divide the slice removed into 2 'wings'; dust with icing sugar and press into cream and jam.

Rock buns: Use basic recipe for 'Cut and come again cake', but add LESS liquid to give a sticky consistency. Divide into about 12 portions. Put on greased baking trays or sheets; sprinkle lightly with sugar and bake for 10–12 minutes towards the top of a hot oven (425–450°F.—Gas Mark 6–7).

A mixer for making icings

Naturally the type of icing determines whether a mixer will be of value to you, but here are ways in which it can save time, effort and physical beating.

1 The blender can be used to sieve the icing sugar if at all lumpy, remember to see the goblet is very dry so no icing sugar sticks round the sides of the goblet.

2 The blender could be used for a water or glacé icing, but some will be wasted whereas the whisk and a bowl enables you to use ALL the icing.

3 The whisk is invaluable for beating icings—in the larger mixers you may find you prefer the beating attachment for large quantities of Royal icing.

Warning: It is possible to over-beat the icing for a royal icing which means you can have large air bubbles in the mixture, so preventing a smooth coating.

Always weigh out the amount of icing sugar and adhere to this, for the most efficient beating of an electric mixer can make you think the icing is very stiff, and there may not be quite enough icing sugar in proportion to the egg whites.

In this case the icing will not harden as much as it should.

The best way of handling the mixer for Royal icing is given under the recipe itself—of course over-beating can occur with glacé icing also, but this is less likely.

American frosting

cooking time	15 minutes (very approximate—for this depends upon the size of saucepan, etc.)
Mixer speed	high

you will need:

6 oz. loaf or granulated sugar	1 egg white
$\frac{1}{4}$ pint water	pinch cream of tartar

1 Put the sugar and water into a saucepan and heat, stirring until the sugar has dissolved.

2 Boil steadily until mixture reaches soft ball stage, i.e. when a little is dropped into cold water, it forms a soft, pliable ball (238°F.).

3 Beat until the syrup turns cloudy, then pour on to the STIFFLY BEATEN egg white.

4 Beat in cream of tartar till mixture thickens. The amount above is sufficient for a good layer on top of a 6-inch cake.

To cover top and sides of a 6-inch cake use 12 oz. sugar, etc.

Flavourings for American frosting

Almond icing: Add 1 teaspoon almond essence to the mixture.

Chocolate icing: Stir in $\frac{1}{2}$ oz. sieved cocoa when the icing reaches 238°F.

Coconut icing: Boil icing until it reaches 238°F.; add 3 oz. desiccated or freshly shredded coconut, stir well, then continue.

Coffee icing: Use 4 tablespoons strong coffee and 4 tablespoons of water.

Jam or jelly icing: Whisk 1 egg white until very stiff, then gradually beat in 2 tablespoons sieved jam or jelly. If possible this should be melted, allowed to cool, but NOT set, before being added. This gives a soft marshmallow type of frosting, which is excellent for sponge cakes, or cakes for children. If the jam or jelly is not melted, you get a slightly mottled effect, but this does not spoil the flavour of the frosting. Continue as before.

Lemon icing: Use 2 tablespoons lemon juice and 6 tablespoons of water to give $\frac{1}{4}$ pint. Also add $\frac{1}{2}$ teaspoon grated lemon rind, if wished.

Orange icing: Use 4 tablespoons fresh orange juice and 4 tablespoons of water and add $\frac{1}{2}$–1 teaspoon very finely grated orange rind.

Pineapple icing: Use either 1 teaspoon pineapple essence in the icing or 4 tablespoons pineapple juice and 4 tablespoons of water.

Seven-minute icing: Put 1 egg white, 3 dessertspoons cold water, 7 oz. granulated sugar and $\frac{1}{4}$ teaspoon cream of tartar into a double saucepan or a basin that fits over a small saucepan. Whisk until well mixed. Place over rapidly boiling water. Beat hard and cook for 7 minutes until frosting stands up in peaks, then add the vanilla essence.

Glacé icing

mixer speed   medium

you will need:

8 oz. icing sugar   approximately 1$\frac{1}{2}$ dessert-
          spoons warm water

1 Sieve the icing sugar, roll between greaseproof paper or put into blender goblet.
2 Either blend in the blender goblet with the water or put into mixing bowl with water and whisk until smooth. The amount above is sufficient for a thin coating on top and sides of a 6-inch cake or for about 12 little cakes.

Flavourings for glacé icing

Almond glacé icing: Add a few drops of almond essence.

Chocolate glacé icing 1: Add 1 good dessertspoon cocoa to the icing and then beat in a knob of butter the size of an acorn, melted.

Chocolate glacé icing 2: You will find it possible to incorporate melted chocolate into glacé icing. On an average use 2 oz. melted chocolate to 8 oz. icing sugar.

Coffee glacé icing: Mix with strong coffee instead of water, or with soluble coffee powder, blended with a little warm water.

Lemon glacé icing: Mix with lemon juice instead of water.

Mocha glacé icing: Add 1 good dessertspoon cocoa to the icing sugar, and use strong coffee instead of water. A small knob of butter, melted, can be added if liked.

Orange glacé icing: Mix with orange juice instead of water.

Spiced glacé icing: Blend $\frac{1}{2}$ teaspoon mixed spice, $\frac{1}{2}$ teaspoon grated nutmeg and $\frac{1}{2}$ teaspoon cinnamon with the icing sugar.

Vanilla glacé icing: Add a few drops of vanilla essence.

Butter icing

First read the remarks about warming the bowl under creaming, etc., for cakes, see page 72, never over-heat the bowl though, otherwise the icing will be 'oily' and spoiled for a time, if this does happen allow mixture to become quite cold, then cream well.

If making a very small quantity as below then make sure the mixer is not working at too high a speed otherwise the butter, etc., will be thrown against the sides of the bowl and time will be wasted in scraping it down.

you will need:

2 oz. butter   flavouring as required
3–4 oz. sieved icing sugar

1 Cream the butter until very soft and white. DO NOT warm it.
2 Work in the sugar and flavouring. To make a firmer icing, use the larger quantity of sugar.
The amount above is sufficient for a filling or topping on a 6-inch cake. To coat top and sides (rather thinly) of a 6-inch cake use 4 oz. butter, etc.; for top, sides and filling use minimum of 6 oz. butter, etc.
This does not allow any extra for piping and butter icing is excellent for this purpose.

Flavourings for butter icing:

Caramel icing: Beat 3 oz. butter. Add approximately 4 tablespoons caramel and 9 oz. sieved icing sugar, alternately, beating the mixture to keep it smooth and fluffy.

Note:

To make the caramel, put 8 oz. granulated sugar and $\frac{1}{4}$ pint water into a small strong pan and stir over gentle heat until the sugar has dissolved. Bring to the boil and boil to a rich golden brown. Use as required. Surplus caramel can always be stored in a bottle and kept for future use.

Chocolate icing: Add a good dessertspoon of chocolate powder or 1 oz. melted chocolate and a few drops vanilla essence to basic butter icing. Recipe page 81.

Coconut icing: Allow 1 oz. desiccated coconut to each 2 oz. butter. Because this is rather dry, use the minimum quantity of icing sugar. It is better to blend the icing first, then add the coconut with a spoon otherwise this tends to cling round the whisk.

Coffee icing: Work in a good dessertspoon of coffee essence or one teaspoon soluble powder dissolved in two teaspoons water. Do this gradually or the mixture will curdle.

Lemon icing: Add 2 teaspoons finely grated lemon rind and gradually beat in 1 dessertspoon lemon juice.

Orange icing: Use 3 teaspoons finely grated orange rind and gradually beat in 1 dessertspoon orange juice.

Rum icing: Add few drops rum essence or about 1 dessertspoon rum.

Vanilla icing: Add half a teaspoon vanilla essence.

Syrup butter cream

cooking time   *approximately* 15 minutes
mixer speed   high then low

you will need:

grated rind of 1 orange or   4 egg yolks
   1 lemon   8 oz. butter
$\frac{1}{4}$ pint water   1 tablespoon orange or
6 oz. loaf or granulated   lemon juice
   sugar

1 Put the grated orange or lemon rind, water and sugar into a pan, stir until the sugar has dissolved, then boil steadily until it reaches

230°F., i.e. a little dropped into cold water forms a thread.
2 Allow to cool slightly, but not set.
3 Meanwhile whisk egg yolks until thick and creamy (use a high speed for this).
4 Gradually beat in the softened butter in small pieces, then the syrup and finally the juice. (Use a low speed for adding butter, syrup, etc.) Allow to cool.

This is enough for a thin layer on top and over sides of an 8-inch cake and 2 layers of filling.

Royal icing

mixer speed   low

you will need:

1 egg white   2 teaspoons lemon juice
8 oz. sieved icing sugar

1 Put the egg white into the dry mixing bowl.
2 Switch on mixer and whisk for a short time— the egg white should not be stiff at all.
3 Gradually add the sugar and lemon juice and then use the lowest speed possible, so preventing the very light sugar from 'flying' in all directions.
4 Increase the speed if wished but a steady movement is better than too rapid whisking which incorporates too many air bubbles, see page 80.
5 Continue whisking until the icing is very white and holds its shape.

The amount above is sufficient for the top only of a 7-inch round cake. Use 1–1$\frac{1}{4}$ lb. icing sugar and all other ingredients in proportion for top and sides of a 7-inch round cake. Use 2 lb. icing sugar and all other ingredients in proportion for top and sides of a 9-inch round cake.

To soften royal icing: Add 1 egg white and 1 tablespoon water to each 1 lb. icing sugar—this is quite adequate for coating cakes but will not hold its shape well for efficient piping OR allow 1 teaspoon glycerine to each 8 oz. icing sugar, this may be added with the lemon juice at Stage 3.

Preserves

There are two ways of using the blender in making jams. When using soft fruit—strawberries, raspberries, etc., put the fruit into the blender and make a purée, cook this for a few minutes THEN add the sugar and proceed as usual. Lemon juice or other flavourings should be added WITH THE SUGAR.

The second method, suitable for harder fruits, is to simmer the fruit for about half the usual time, until beginning to soften; then put the fruit and liquid into the blender and make a purée. Because the cooking time will be shorter when adopting this method, less water than usual may be used, i.e. approximately half the amount given in a standard recipe.

This means you will have a shorter boiling time when the sugar has been dissolved, so the jam should have a better colour as well as flavour.

Raspberry jam

1 lb. raspberries   1 lb. sugar (preferably preserving or loaf)

Put the fruit into the blender goblet and switch gradually to low speed until a smooth purée. Continue until all the fruit has been used. Tip into the preserving pan or saucepan, heat gently for a few minutes (this extracts the pectin), then stir in the sugar over a low heat until thoroughly dissolved. Boil quickly until setting point is reached.

1 lb. sugar produces $1\frac{2}{3}$ lb. jam.

Blackcurrant jam

1 lb. blackcurrants $1\frac{1}{4}$ lb. sugar (preferably
just over $\frac{1}{4}$ pint water   loaf or preserving)

1 Put the blackcurrants and water into the blender and switch on until a smooth purée, continue like this until all the fruit has been emulsified.
2 Put into the preserving pan or saucepan and

simmer gently until the fruit is hot—blackcurrant jam is an ideal one in which to make use of the blender for it obviates any possibility of tough skins.
3 Test to see that any minute particles of skin ARE soft.
4 Add the sugar and stir over a low heat until thoroughly dissolved.
5 Boil rapidly until setting point is reached.
   $1\frac{1}{4}$ lb. sugar produces just over 2 lb. jam.

Fruit with stones

If fruit has stones, such as damsons and plums, then it should be put through the sieving attachment on the mixer or the stones must be removed before using the blender.

Mincemeat

Many people like a mincemeat where all the ingredients are minced to give a moist purée, rather than whole ingredients. Use the mincer or the blender.

Before putting into the goblet or through the mincer:
a Stone raisins (unless using seedless kind).
b Peel and core apple and blanch nuts.

you will need for approximately $2\frac{1}{2}$ lb.:

4 oz. shredded suet or melted margarine	4 oz. mixed peel finely grated rind and juice of 1 large lemon
4 oz. grated apple	1 teaspoon mixed spice
1 lb. mixed dried fruit	$\frac{1}{2}$ teaspoon cinnamon
4 oz. sugar, preferably demerara	$\frac{1}{2}$ teaspoon grated nutmeg
4 oz. blanched and well dried almonds	4 tablespoons brandy, whisky or rum

1 Mix all the ingredients together.
2 Put into dry jam jars and cover thoroughly.
3 Leave in a cool, dry place.

Do not cut down on the quantities of sugar, fat or spirit if you wish this to keep well. Make quite certain the fruit is dry. If this has been washed, let it dry for at least 24 hours before making mincemeat.

Marmalade

Any favourite marmalade recipe can be used. If a *mincer attachment* is available this can be used, but obviously a fine *shredder attachment* gives more 'elegant' strips of peel. If neither is available then use the blender attachment.
The following recipe is a good 'basic' one, which produces a moderately sweet marmalade.

Seville orange marmalade

1 lb. Seville oranges   juice 1 large lemon
3 pints water
3 lb. sugar (preferably
   loaf or preserving)

1 Cut away the peel from the oranges, having washed the fruit thoroughly in cold water.
2 **WITH A MINCER:** Put the peel through this using the fine or coarse plates depending upon personal taste.
WITH A SHREDDER: Put the peel through this until evenly shredded.
WITH A BLENDER: Put the peel and enough water to cover into the goblet, switch on until finely cut.
3 Put the peel into a bowl with the cold water; squeeze out the orange juice and put this into a separate container.
4 Tie the pips into a muslin bag and add to the water, together with the fruit pith which must be used, as this, plus the pips, adds flavour as well as setting quality.
5 Soak overnight, then simmer gently until the peel is very tender.
6 Stir in the sugar, and continue stirring until dissolved. Add the orange juice and lemon juice and boil rapidly until the marmalade sets.
3 lb. sugar produces 5 lb. marmalade.

Beverages of all kinds

One of the most helpful uses of a blender (liquidiser) is to prepare a selection of hot or cold drinks. This is ideal for children or adults and is particularly valuable in giving interest and flavour to milk, which is such an important food for growing children, invalids and the elderly.

Milk Shakes and Beverages

It is possible to make a great variety of drinks with the help of the blender. You can combine acid fresh fruits and milk without fear of curdling, since the action of the blades is so rapid they emulsify the ingredients in seconds. Drinks are deliciously light when mixed in the blender. Put the hot or cold ingredients in together and switch on.
Warning: If using ice, do not use too large pieces because, in time, they can harm the blades. Do not overfill the goblet with the ingredients.

Make sure the lid is very firmly in position and hold this as you switch on.
Warm the blender before adding very hot mixtures.

Crushed ice

It is probably 'safer' and certainly kinder to the blades in a blender goblet if ice is crushed for drinks.
To crush ice: Put the cubes into a clean tea cloth and cover with the cloth, then crush firmly with a rolling pin.
In the case of a large blender the manufacturers may advocate using this for crushing ice; follow their directions.

Cold Milk Shakes

Because acid fruit and milk are emulsified so quickly, you get no signs of curdling. It is important, however, to serve the drink straight away.

All quantities given are for one glass

Almond milk shake

Put $\frac{3}{4}$ of a tumbler of cold milk plus a few drops of almond essence, a spoonful of vanilla ice cream and $\frac{1}{2}$ tablespoon blanched almonds with sugar to taste into the blender goblet. Switch gradually to high until light and fluffy.

Banana milk shake

Put $\frac{1}{2}$ a banana, a squeeze of lemon juice, $\frac{1}{2}$ a tumbler of milk and a spoonful of ice cream or a little crushed ice into the goblet, switch gradually to high, leave until light and fluffy.

Cherry milk shake

Put a few ripe cherries *with stones removed* into the goblet with a little sugar, crushed ice or a spoonful of ice cream and $\frac{1}{2}$ a tumbler of milk. Switch gradually to high, leave until light and fluffy.

In winter-time, use well-drained canned cherries.

Egg milk shake

Put an egg, a spoonful of ice cream, sugar to taste and $\frac{1}{2}$ a tumbler of cold milk into the goblet, switch gradually to high, leave until light and fluffy.

Lemon milk shake

Put about $\frac{1}{2}$–1 tablespoon lemon juice, sugar to taste and $\frac{3}{4}$ of a tumbler of milk into the goblet. Add either a little crushed ice or better still, a spoonful of ice cream. Switch gradually to high, leave until light and fluffy.

Orange milk shake

Cut the pulp from a fresh orange, discarding pith and pips. Put into the goblet with a little crushed ice or a tablespoon ice cream and $\frac{1}{2}$ a tumbler of milk. Sugar is not necessary for most people. Switch gradually to high, leave until light and fluffy.

Tangerines are equally delicious.

Ovaltine milk shake

Put a very little crushed ice into the goblet, together with $\frac{3}{4}$ of a tumbler of cold milk, sugar and Ovaltine to taste. Switch gradually to high, leave until light and fluffy.

Raspberry milk shake

Put 1–2 tablespoons fresh raspberries with a little sugar, a spoonful of ice cream or a little crushed ice and $\frac{1}{2}$ a tumbler of cold milk into the goblet. Switch gradually to high until light and fluffy.

Other berry fruits—blackcurrants, strawberries, redcurrants, loganberries, etc.—are equally successful.

Rose hip milk shake

Put the required quantity of rose hip syrup (remember it is very concentrated and rather sweet) into the goblet, together with $\frac{3}{4}$ of a tumbler of cold milk, a little crushed ice or a spoonful of ice cream. Switch gradually to high, leave until light and fluffy.

Syrups

There are many excellent milk shake syrups on the market, obtainable from grocers and stores. These are designed for flavouring milk shakes. Remember they are very concentrated so do not exceed the recommended amount.

Be very careful, when making milk shakes, that the goblet is not over-filled and that the lid is firmly in position.

Creamy whips and flips

Creamy egg nog

blender speed   high

you will need for 1 glass:

1 egg	sugar to taste
$\frac{1}{4}$ pint cold milk	

to decorate:
1 tablespoon whipped
  cream or ice cream

1 Put all ingredients into blender goblet and switch gradually to high.
2 Leave for about 30 seconds or until light and fluffy.
3 Put into an ice-cold tumbler and top with the whipped or ice cream.

Note:

A little crushed ice may be added at Stage 1—but read note page 84.

Brandy egg flip

blender speed   high

you will need for 1 glass:

1 egg   ¼ pint cold milk
1 tablespoon brandy   sugar to taste

Method as Creamy egg nog.

Iced chocolate

blender speed   high

you will need for 1 glass:

1 good teaspoon cocoa   ¾ tumbler cold milk
  with 1 teaspoon sugar   few drops vanilla essence
  OR   few crushed ice cubes
2 heaped teaspoons   whipped cream (optional)
  chocolate with
  1 teaspoon sugar

1 Put all ingredients except cream into blender
  goblet with the crushed ice.
2 Switch gradually to high for 30 seconds.
3 Top with a little lightly whipped cream.

Iced coffee whip

Put a few small ice cubes or crushed ice into
the goblet, add ¼ pint strong coffee and a
spoonful of vanilla ice cream and switch on
until smoothly blended. Serve in a tall glass
topped with a 'blob' of whipped cream.

To vary:

Add ½ teaspoon cinnamon.
Omit the ice cream, add ½ pint thin cream or
evaporated milk.
Add 2 teaspoons cocoa to the coffee, etc.

Fresh fruit drinks

All the drinks are sufficient for one tall glass:

Note:

Fruits like apples will discolour if left out in
the air, so prepare just before serving.

Apple cooler

blender speed   high

½ dessert apple   ¼ pint lemonade
¼ pint ginger ale   little ice

1 Peel the apple and put into the blender with
  the ale and lemonade and ice.
2 Switch on until light and frothy.

Peach glory

blender speed   high

you will need for 2 glasses:

1 medium-sized ripe   2 tablespoons strawberry
  peach or 2 canned peach   ice cream
  halves   ½ pint soda water
1 tablespoon fresh lemon
  juice
little sugar with fresh
  peaches if wished

1 Skin the fresh peach, then put with all the
  ingredients into the blender.
2 Switch on until blended and light and fluffy.

Banana lemon whip

blender speed   high

1 small banana or   nearly ½ pint lemonade or
  ½ larger one   diluted lemon squash or
spoonful ice cream   use little fresh lemon
                               juice and water with
                               sugar to taste

1 Put the peeled banana and all the other
  ingredients into the blender.
2 Switch on until light and fluffy. If preferred the
  ice cream may be put on top of the drink
  rather than being blended with it.

Lemon fizz

blender speed   high

you will need for 2 glasses:

1 large lemon   ½ pint soda water
2 spoonfuls vanilla ice
  cream

1 Peel the lemon, remove the pulp and put this
  into the blender.
2 Add the ice cream and soda water.
3 Switch on until light and fluffy, taste and add a
  very little sugar before removing from the
  goblet if wished.
  Lemon Ginger: Use ginger ale or ginger beer
  instead of soda water.

Apricot orange

blender speed   high

4 cooked or canned   3 tablespoons syrup from
  apricot halves   cooking the fruit or the
juice 2 oranges   canned fruit
                              few ice cubes

1 Put all the ingredients into the blender and
  switch on until blended.

Prune orange

Use cooked or canned prunes and some of the syrup instead of apricot syrup as in apricot orange. (Remove the stones from the prunes.) This makes a most delicious drink.

Prune orange cream

blender speed	high

you will need for 2 glasses:

6 stoned, cooked or canned prunes	2 tablespoons vanilla ice cream
juice 2 medium oranges	few ice cubes

1 Put all the ingredients into the blender.
2 Switch on until well blended and light and fluffy.
This is an excellent drink for invalids.
TRY other combinations of fruit, etc., for yourself.

Party drinks

A blender is an ideal means of providing unusual drinks—in fact it is one method of entertaining your guests to let *them* prepare their own party drinks.
If you have no cocktail shaker then use the blender goblet instead—read the comments on page 84 about using ice cubes though.
The following recipes are typical of mixed drinks, try your own combination of flavours.

Advocaat flip

blender speed	high

you will need for 2 glasses:

3 tablespoons advocaat	juice 2 fresh oranges
little crushed ice	

1 Put the ingredients into the blender.
2 Switch on until blended, then pour into 2 Martini glasses.

Cherry Brandy sling

blender speed	high

you will need for 2 glasses:

2 measures of Cherry Brandy	little crushed ice
2 measures of dry white wine	

to decorate:
twists of lemon peel

1 Put all the ingredients into the blender and switch to high for a few seconds only.
2 Put into glasses and top with twists of lemon peel.

Lemon Manhattan

blender speed	high

you will need for 2–3 glasses:

1 fresh lemon	dash Angostura bitters
2 measures of whisky	about 1 tablespoon curaçao
2 measures of a dry vermouth	little crushed ice

1 Take several pieces lemon rind from the fruit then squeeze out the juice.
2 Put this and all the other ingredients into the blender and switch to high for a few seconds only.
3 Pour into 2 or 3 cocktail glasses.

Fresh tomato cocktail

blender speed	high

you will need for 2 glasses:

4 large ripe tomatoes	pinch cayenne pepper
little crushed ice	dash celery salt
1–2 teaspoons Worcestershire sauce	pinch sugar, preferably brown
	1 tablespoon lemon juice

to top:
lemon peel

1 Skin and de-seed the tomatoes—in this way straining is not necessary OR put the tomatoes with the skins and seeds into the blender goblet then strain afterwards.
2 Add all the ingredients to the tomatoes and switch on until smoothly blended.
3 Strain if necessary, see Stage 1.
4 Serve in cocktail glasses, topped with a twist of lemon peel.

Children's dishes & preparing babies' food

Many of the recipes in this book are ideal for children.

For example, the meat dishes using a mincer, etc., enable a busy mother to prepare the food for young children within a matter of minutes. Simply take the cooked meat from the family joint, etc., and put it into the blender with a little of the gravy. A small child may then feed itself.

The desserts and puddings will appeal to most children and they are good for children since they contain important foods—eggs, milk, etc. Many children dislike milk, and the range of milk shakes will make it much more inviting.

Preparing foods for a baby:—

Main meal—When a baby is first given meat, vegetables, etc., it is essential that these are made into a very smooth purée. The blender goblet is ideal for emulsifying meat with stock and/or vegetables. Follow the directions found on page 15 under Soups.

Remember that a baby must have very fresh food, so do not emulsify too much of any one ingredient. It is better to cook this freshly and emulsify and then serve it to the child. Should any food be left, cover it carefully and store for one day only in the refrigerator.

Dessert—It is very important that a child has as big a variety of foods as possible from a very early age, and many adult dishes may be made suitable for children if put into the blender to give a very smooth purée.

If a child dislikes a food such as egg custard, emulsify this with a little freshly cooked fruit.

The strong flavour of cooked prunes is made much milder if this is emulsified with cold custard or cold milk pudding.

Beef and vegetable broth: Put a good beef bone into a saucepan with water to cover and a little seasoning. Simmer for about 2 hours—or use shin of beef.

Strain off this stock and put it back into a pan with a carrot, and a potato.

Simmer until nearly soft, then add a little green vegetable and continue cooking, then put into the blender.

Peas, or beans may be used—also soaked dried beans, but care must be taken not to give very small children (just beginning mixed feeding) indigestible vegetables such as onions. Some babies may find peas indigestible so use a small amount only. Vary the vegetables used in this broth so the child becomes accustomed to a new taste.

Fruit purées for babies: When a baby is very small many fruits are not advisable—your Health Visitor or Clinic or Doctor will give specialised advice, but generally speaking a child under two years should NOT BE GIVEN: Strawberries and raspberries and blackcurrants (they may have blackcurrant syrup of course), unless these are sieved most carefully so there is no sign of any pips—even so it is better to leave these fruits until after a year.

Currants, raisins, sultanas in any form unless made into a purée.

Cherries tend to be indigestible for small children.

Fruits a baby may have when put on to mixed feeding:

cooked or raw apple

bananas—if really ripe

cooked prunes—if well sieved

little pear if well cooked or ripe—do not give too much as it is an indigestible fruit

citrus fruits (as well as juice)—remove all pith, skin and pips.

To serve the fruit: If serving the fruit with custard it can be emulsified with the custard, this means small pieces of raw apple or pear can be put into the blender with the custard.

If serving cooked fruit then the fruit and juice from cooking may be emulsified together and served with a custard or the fruit purée left in the blender, the custard added, and the two emulsified together.

Instead of custard use cooked rice pudding or other milk puddings.

Invalid dishes

When someone is ill it is always difficult to tempt their appetite, and the following ideas should be helpful to an invalid.

Someone who is ill needs:—

a Protein in the form of meat or poultry, fish or chicken, eggs and cheese. At the same time the protein should be in an easy-to-digest form. Many of the recipes in this book are admirably suited for invalids.

b Iron: This is obtainable from liver, watercress, treacle—the recipe below gives an appetising way of serving liver.

c Milk in the form of drinks, custards, desserts, home-made ice cream and milk shakes; these are often an excellent way of having milk in an appetising form. Milk and cheese provide calcium, which is very necessary for children and adults and particularly important for the elderly.

d Fats: Obviously invalids, unless they are on a fat-free diet, need a certain amount of fat but this should not be given excessively since it can prove difficult to digest.

e Carbohydrates: Sugar and starches are less necessary to an invalid.

f Vitamins: A very important vitamin to an invalid is Vitamin C, and the maximum of Vitamin C is retained in fruits and vegetables that contain this when a blender is used. The reason is that fruits and vegetables are cooked more lightly than usual and it is overcooking that destroys so much of this very necessary vitamin.

There are, of course, many other vitamins and minerals essential to invalids as well as people who are in good health but those stated above are of particular interest in this book dealing with mixers.

You will notice that recipes are for 4 people, this is because it is often easier to combine an invalid dish with a family dish.

Liver soufflé

cooking time	40 minutes
mincer speed	medium
mixer speed	high

you will need for 4 servings:

8–10 oz. calf's liver	$\frac{1}{4}$ pint milk
1 oz. butter	3 eggs
1 oz. flour	seasoning

1 Put the liver through the fine plate of the mincer. If you do not possess a mincing attachment it can be put into the blender with the milk, but this is less satisfactory.*

2 Heat the butter, stir in the flour and cook for several minutes.

3 Gradually blend in the milk or milk and liver, bring to the boil and cook until thickened.

4 Add the egg yolks, seasoning.

5 Meanwhile, whisk the egg whites until very stiff. Put the minced liver into the sauce, then the egg whites; blend gently but thoroughly. Put into 4 individual soufflé dishes and bake for 20–25 minutes just above the centre of a moderately hot oven (375°F.—Gas Mark 5).

*It means the liver is partially cooked with the sauce.

Liver cream

Ingredients as for the liver soufflé, but add the whole eggs, do not beat the whites, then stir in 2 oz. soft breadcrumbs.

Put into a greased 1–1½ lb. loaf tin, cover with buttered paper and bake in the centre of a very moderate oven (325–350°F.—Gas Mark 3) for approximately 50 minutes.

If the loaf tin is put into another tin or dish of cold water it makes certain that the sides of the mixture do not become dry and hard.

Chicken soufflé

Use minced uncooked chicken in place of liver and chicken stock in place of milk in the liver soufflé recipe.

Lightly cooked chicken could be used for an invalid, but this is not advisable for someone suffering from gastric disorders since 'twice-cooked' food is generally forbidden.

Invalid fruit condé

cooking time	few minutes
blender speed	high
mixer speed	low

you will need for 4 servings:

small can fruit or cooked fruit	few tablespoons thick cream
medium can creamed rice or about ¾ pint rice pudding	

for the glaze:

3–4 tablespoons redcurrant jelly	3–4 tablespoons water

1 Put the fruit into the blender and switch on to make a smooth thick purée, use only as much syrup from the can or juice from cooking the fruit as necessary.
2 Tip out the fruit and if wishing to have a very smooth rice mixture put this into the blender with the cream and make a purée.
3 If you do not particularly want a very smooth rice mixture whip the cream lightly with the mixer and fold this into the rice.
4 Put the rice into a serving dish and top with the fruit purée.
5 Heat the jelly and water together until the jelly has melted.
This dessert can be served hot or cold, so if serving cold allow the jelly mixture to cool slightly then spread over the fruit.
If serving hot then pour the jelly over the hot fruit, etc., and serve at once.
Other milk puddings can be used instead, i.e. semolina, tapioca, etc.

Quick and easy desserts for invalids

1 **Baked cored apples:** Slit the skins round the centre before cooking so they are easy to remove. When soft remove the skins and coat the apples with meringue—to cover 4 medium-sized apples you need 2–3 egg whites and 2–3 oz. sugar if serving hot or 4–6 oz. sugar if serving cold—see directions on pages 52 and 75 for making and baking meringues.
2 **Rice jelly:** Make ¾ pint rice pudding or use canned creamed rice. Put into the blender. Dissolve a 1 pint lemon jelly in ½ pint only of very hot water, add to the rice mixture. Switch on until blended then pour into individual dishes. Serves 4–5.
3 **Crumb custard:** Make crumbs from sponge cake or sweet biscuits or ginger nut biscuits or macaroons—allow 2–3 oz. to 1 pint milk, 2–3 eggs and sugar to taste. Keep the crumbs in the blender and add the milk, switch on until mixed, pour on to beaten eggs and sugar. Bake as egg custard.
4 **Milk pudding soufflé:** Make an ordinary milk pudding, cooking until fairly stiff. Put into blender with 2 egg yolks, little extra sugar and a little chopped fruit (apricots, apples, pears, etc.). Whisk 2 egg whites until very stiff, fold into the pudding mixture and bake for approximately 35 minutes in a moderate oven (375°F. —Gas Mark 4–5).

Gastric sufferers

Unfortunately many people suffer from some gastric disorder and this means a prolonged and fairly strict diet. It is important that foods given should contain no irritants in the form of skin, pips, etc., so that a sieve attachment on a mixer is absolutely ideal.

A blender (liquidiser), however, is excellent in providing smooth purée from many fruits and vegetables.

A mincing attachment on a mixer will also be useful in mincing meat or poultry when this is allowed in the diet.

Health-giving ideas

I hope you will enjoy making the recipes in this book. If you analyse them you will find that they are basically very simple but made more interesting by the use of a mixer. Many of them are based on essential and health-giving foods.

If you are planning a special health diet you will find the juice separator of immense value, for this enables you to extract the juice, not only from fruits such as apples, pears, etc., as well as citrus fruits, but also from a range of vegetables and herbs such as parsley. Be adventurous about mixing these juices, for example:—

Beetroot and orange juice: extract juice from raw or cooked beetroot, blend with orange juice and a little seasoning. This is a slightly sweet drink.

Carrot and parsley: extract the juice from young raw carrots and add just enough parsley juice to give a pleasant 'bite'.

Cabbage and chive: extract the juice from cabbage and either chives or spring onions, season well.

Spinach and onion: extract the juice from spinach with a very little onion—this is also extremely good if blended with a little lemon juice.

The above are suggestions only, but try a wide range of flavours—all of which are good for you, as well as good to eat.

Note for slimmers

Remember many of the recipes for desserts, etc., in this book can be prepared using sugar substitutes in place of sugar.

Make sauces from cooked or raw vegetables without any flour thickening—this makes so many plainly cooked foods (meat, fish, etc.) more palatable.

You can eat soups on a slimming diet if you make these from low calorie vegetables then put them into the blender and make a purée WITHOUT USING FAT OR THICKENING —naturally this will depend upon your particular diet—some cut down on liquids— others on fat—but most slimming diets cut out carbohydrates in the form of flour and sugar.